Shakespeare
in Action

Shakespeare in Action

30 Theatre Makers on Their Practice

Jaq Bessell

THE ARDEN SHAKESPEARE

LONDON • NEW YORK • OXFORD • NEW DELHI • SYDNEY

THE ARDEN SHAKESPEARE
Bloomsbury Publishing Plc
50 Bedford Square, London, WC1B 3DP, UK
1385 Broadway, New York, NY 10018, USA

BLOOMSBURY, THE ARDEN SHAKESPEARE and the Arden Shakespeare
logo are trademarks of Bloomsbury Publishing Plc

First published in Great Britain 2019
Reprinted in 2019

Cover design by Maria Rajka
Cover images: (middle) rehearsal image of *Coriolanus*, photo by Helen
Maybanks © RSC; (background): close-up of a page containing the third
act of William Shakespeare's *The Tragedy of Othello, the Moor of Venice*, ©
Marco Venturini Autieri / Getty Images

A catalogue record for this book is available from the British Library.

Library of Congress Cataloging-in-Publication Data
Names: Bessell, Jacquelyn, 1967- author.
Title: Shakespeare in action : 30 theatre makers on their practice / Jaq Bessell.
Description: London, UK ; New York, NY : The Arden Shakespeare, 2019. |
Includes bibliographical references and index.
Identifiers: LCCN 2018055711 (print) | LCCN 2018058712 (ebook) | ISBN
9781474229753 (ePub) | ISBN 9781474229760 (ePDF) |
ISBN 9781350033504 (hardback) | ISBN 9781408171738(paperback)
Subjects: LCSH: Shakespeare, William, 1564-1616–Dramatic production. |
Actors–Interviews.
Classification: LCC PR3091 (ebook) | LCC PR3091 .B477 2019 (print) | DDC
792.02–dc23
LC record available at https://lccn.loc.gov/2018055711

ISBN: HB: 978-1-350-03350-4
PB: 978-1-4081-7173-8
ePDF: 978-1-4742-2976-0
eBook: 978-1-4742-2975-3

Typeset by Newgen KnowledgeWorks Pvt. Ltd., Chennai, India
Printed and bound in Great Britain

To find out more about our authors and books visit www.bloomsbury.com
and sign up for our newsletters.

For Lindsay Kemp (1938–2018)
and Ken Washington (1946–2014)

CONTENTS

Creatives

Conclusions 175

ACKNOWLEDGEMENTS

I would like to thank the thirty practitioners I interviewed about their work, for generously giving their time and insights to this volume. Tom Berkeley, Lorna Burslem, Anne Catchpole, Al Coppola, Craig McKenzie and Ross White gave invaluable help in preparing transcripts of the interviews in this volume, and to them I am most grateful. Niall Bailey and other colleagues at the Guildford School of Acting, as well as former colleagues and students at the Shakespeare Institute (University of Birmingham) in Stratford upon Avon, provided me with encouragement along the way. My editors, Margaret Bartley and Mark Dudgeon, have been gracious and patient, and I am grateful for the kindness and assistance provided by Lara Bateman, Ian Buck and the team at Bloomsbury Publishing. Finally, I would like to thank Jan and Rosie Knightley for their love and support.

Introduction

This is a practical book revealing the processes and practices that the cast (actors) and creatives (directors, designers and coaches) working at some of the larger producing theatres in the United Kingdom and the United States use, when preparing and performing Shakespeare's plays. The diverse theatre practices and methodologies in this volume are presented 'from the horse's mouth', and I hope that the collective wisdom and experience represented in the interviews will offer readers new insights, and different ways of reading Shakespeare in performance, from the inside out. It is written primarily for non-practitioners with an academic interest in how Shakespeare's plays are brought to the stage, but I hope the book will also be of interest to actors in training and to other theatre practitioners.

During my tenure at the Shakespeare Institute in Stratford upon Avon, I became aware that many intelligent and critical students of Shakespeare in performance were looking at performances of productions at their partner institution, the RSC, from different perspectives to those of the people who made those productions. When analysing performances in papers I was obliged to mark, students tended to do so from a product-oriented, rather than process-oriented perspective. As most of these students would have little prospect of gaining access to rehearsals for RSC productions, and few if any had any prior experience of actor training methodologies, I found it difficult to imagine how the situation could be otherwise. What became clear to me was that there was no dearth of interest in those behind-the-scenes processes on the part of those students, in fact they were hungry for first-hand evidence of the working processes of the practitioners whose work they admired. Since leaving the Shakespeare Institute and working within the conservatoire sector, I have encountered a different constituency of students, those embarking on actor training programmes at undergraduate and postgraduate level, who are obliged to write essays reflecting on their own practice, and locate it in a recognizable professional context. It is my hope that *Shakespeare in Action* will serve both constituencies. The interviews in this volume will open up several strands of theatre practice to both kinds of reader, and, I hope, provide these readers with clear and appropriate language with which one might appraise performances on the stage or on the screen. The interviews allow the practitioners themselves to unpack key concepts for non-practitioners, as well as inviting more experienced readers to use this evidence to follow their own research agenda. At the very least, *Shakespeare in Action* should provide students of Shakespeare in performance with an enhanced technical vocabulary with which to read performance evidence, and supply actors in training with a wealth of first-hand evidence to enable them to select the juicy quotation they need to include in whatever essay they may be obliged to write.

In *Shakespeare in the Theatre: Mark Rylance at the Globe* (2017) Stephen Purcell examines the work of many of the contributors to this volume, and draws on primary evidence from the Globe Research Bulletins I wrote as the Globe's head of research during Rylance's tenure as artistic director. As it will become clear quickly to the reader, Purcell and I both consider the first decade of Globe productions to be groundbreaking, for similar reasons. I hope that this book will be read alongside Purcell's, and that the broader scope of this book – encompassing not just Globe productions, but those at the major institutions on both sides of the Atlantic – will invite readers to make fruitful comparisons between the major stakeholders in the Shakespeare 'industry' today.

The principle of action

Two of the working titles I considered for this book (but ultimately rejected) were *The Shakespeare Ensemble* and *The Principle of Action*. The reasons are appropriately twofold: (a) ensemble work brings together individuals with specific skills, experiences and expertise, whose work is guided by a common principle or goal, and (b) a common principle of *action* underpins the interviews that follow. I suggest that the principle of action is the smallest unit of performance, and as any actor will tell you, 'action' is the lingua franca of rehearsal and performance. Jade Anouka sums up why this is so:

> Shakespeare's poetic language is potentially a bit overwhelming, and I find the most useful approach for me is to take these very big, rich ideas, and to try to boil them down to the simplest, strongest action I can … [t]hat can help keep you focussed on what you are trying to *do* to the other person … your character is *saying* all of this, but it helps to ask: 'what am I actually trying to *achieve*? (p. 22)

An action is *playable*, whereas a theme, or a contextual footnote, may not always be. Alex Hassell's interview also describes how close-reading for actions may differ from other ways of reading a Shakespeare text: 'Usually when I'm looking at a script what I'm trying to see with a line is: Why am I saying that line? What am I trying to change about the other person by saying that line? What is wrong with them or with this situation that needs to be changed by me saying the line?' (p. 43). As such, I would argue that critical readers of Shakespeare in performance should consider this emphasis on *action*, on the 'doing' of performance, when evaluating performances of Shakespeare's plays.

Hamlet may have coined the best advice for the actor –
'Suit the action to the word, the word to the action' – but it
was Stanislavski who was to later brand the name of *action*
indelibly on the hearts of generations of actors in training.
Stanislavski's system of psycho-physical actions continues to
underpin the language of modern actor training, as Jonathan
McGuinness notes:

> I think almost all modern actors have been influenced by
> Stanislavski, even if they believe that they are in no way,
> shape or form a Method actor or a Stanislavski follower.
> That's because it is what we all do now, it's ingrained
> through training and experience: we all ask, 'Why am
> I doing this?' and regardless of what you call them, you play
> objectives in some way. I think actors have probably always
> done this, but Stanislavski formulated a method around
> those practices. (pp. 62–3)

Performances, and indeed every directorial or design aspect of a
given production, are composed of a sequence of many actions;
each action is also a choice made by an actor or a creative, and
each choice has significant potential to affect what we think
we are talking about when we talk about theatre. Designers
and directors can give full consideration to the sequence of
actions that make up the shape of a production as a whole,
whereas performers necessarily concern themselves primarily
with single actions and reactions in turn, each in its own
moment of performance. At one end of the spectrum, an action
can be discovered spontaneously as a response to external
stimuli, as in a moment of pure improvisation between two
actors. Jonathan McGuinness describes why these moments
are important, and why an actor should not fix their choice of
actions in advance of group rehearsals:

> Shakespeare was an actor, writing for other actors who he
> knew. You can really tell that when you work on it. For me,
> 99 per cent of rehearsal is about being in the moment with

the other actor, discovering what is happening dramatically …
It's out of those moments that unique moments emerge, and
those are the things specific to the rehearsal room, they aren't
something that you can predict from working alone. (pp. 64–5)

At the other end of the spectrum, an action may be orchestrated
in a very explicit way, as in choreographed movement, or stage
combat. For the latter activity, the spontaneous responses
Jonathan describes above are neither appropriate nor in
line with health and safety legislation: rather, in the case of
orchestrated actions, the strong communication of intention,
played out in a clear and committed physical action, can carry
the storytelling in ways that keep the actors safe, and obviate
the need for spoken text. In between these two extremes
lies the majority of action-practices used by performers of
Shakespeare in rehearsal and performance.

Actions may be identified in the text by the actor while
reading the script, and learning the lines, but action choices
identified early in the process will typically undergo a process
of radical or subtle modification, over the course of the
rehearsal process and the life of the production. This process of
modifying actions is usually prompted by the actions of scene
partners, and the changing conditions of performance. Pippa
Nixon's interview describes this process of 'acting as reacting':

At some point in the rehearsal period, you have to be
mechanical and go: 'Right – I have to make some very strong
choices here' … First you have to invest in those choices, but
then when someone plays something towards me, I want
to be able to respond to that, rather than fit their actions
into the mechanics of what I've already built. Things have
to be able to change. It's no good getting stuck in a choice
that you have made … lots of discoveries are made through
'play'. (pp. 66–7)

It is therefore the choice and type of action itself which
determines meaning, on a moment by moment basis, and Jade

Anouka describes how unique and specific combinations of actions in turn produce unique and specific performances. For Jade, actions are

> how we get so much variety: it is so interesting to see different people play the same part, because they will have chosen such different actions. You can't play a role the same way as anyone else, because even though your objectives may be the same as another actor in the same role, you will have chosen different actions on the way to pursue those objectives. So that's why each performance is unique. (pp. 23–4)

The model of reading performance described by Jade has been formed by her experience as an actor in training, and it has been reinforced in her professional life by the experience of working with other theatre professionals who share this approach. As a director and teacher of acting in theatres, professional training programmes and conservatoires across the United States and the United Kingdom, I am interested in the way that Stanislavski's system continues to have value in modern actor training, in ways that it would be hard to imagine (for example) a literary critical work published in 1936 continuing to dominate Shakespeare Studies today. The key to the system's success is, as Jonathan McGuinness notes, its emphasis on action, on doing: 'it is what we all *do* now' (p. 63; emphasis mine), and its proven ability to be adapted or applied in a diverse range of creative contexts. These interviews unpack and identify various types of actions at the core of modern Shakespearean production, used by practitioners from a variety of training and performance backgrounds.

Tim Carroll 'challenge[s] the assumption that literary critics of Shakespeare *need* to take performance into account more' (p. 103; emphasis in the original), but I would argue that it is important to recognize some of the practical and technical methodologies underpinning Shakespearean performance, whether it is experienced live, via archival evidence, or mediated through print. At the risk of drawing a clumsy parallel, not all students of art history would profess to have an aptitude for painting, but few of them would feel comfortable discussing a famous painting without a basic understanding of how the painting was made: the materials used, the composition of the painting and the quality of the brushstrokes are elements which inform the way an art history student would look at and respond to a painting, alongside other vital contextual information relating to the tradition to which the painting belongs. If a basic technical vocabulary enhances the art history student's appreciation of the work of art, I hope that some of the widely disseminated actor training principles discussed in the interviews will enhance the Shakespeare Studies reader's appreciation of the compositional elements of modern Shakespearean performance.

Taken as a whole, the interviews should also provide the reader with a sense of how, for example, the actions of the director may function in relation to those of the voice coach, the actor, and so on within a modern Shakespeare ensemble. The interviews unpack specific practitioners' methods, acknowledging the influence of key institutions (including Shakespeare's Globe, the Royal Shakespeare Company, the Shakespeare Theatre and others) while at the same time resisting some of the more general assumptions about institutional 'house styles', which tend to blur the distinctions between different methodologies which coexist productively within so many Shakespeare-producing theatres. That said, the reader should not overlook some methodological principles common to many apparently diverse institutions separated by history, geography and commercial sector. What the respondents identify as 'layers' of work – phases in preparation, rehearsal and performance – are partly inflected by the institutional practices of different producing organizations, partly by training regimes and partly by specific circumstances encountered by the practitioner. Reading for these areas of influence, the reader will make connections between practitioners across disciplines.

I asked each respondent to describe their 'action' with or on a Shakespeare play. To the director, action may mean something slightly different: the play can happen in front of, or 'to' the audience. For the designer, it is quite normal to talk about what the design is 'doing', rather than the way it looks or sounds. Director Polly Findlay describes how her reading of the action of *As You Like It* informed every creative decision she and her team made in rehearsal and production: 'if the play was to perform a transitive action on the audience, it should be "to delight them". So, as the editing decisions had to relate the driving line of the sentence I just mentioned, so the tech and production decisions had to be built around the idea of wanting to delight the audience' (p. 124). I would suggest that in various ways, action is the lingua franca of the many creative processes which lead to productions being made. Therefore, it seems reasonable to suggest that audiences and readers of Shakespeare in performance might also consider using the language of action when evaluating productions, whether live or recorded.

How this book came together

I have enjoyed an eclectic career to date, working mostly in theatres or conservatoires, and briefly in research-focused higher education contexts. As I mention above, while working at the Shakespeare Institute between 2009 and 2013 I became more aware of a range of literary-critical approaches to Shakespeare's texts, and I was particularly struck by the significance performance evidence (live or recorded) held for performance historians, textual editors, educators and a host of other branches of what might be called the Shakespeare 'subject area'. What was equally striking was the openness with which these expert readers embraced practical approaches to Shakespeare's language. This led me to re-examine a few unhelpful preconceptions I'd been carrying around, about 'critical' versus 'practical' uses of Shakespeare, after which

I concluded that the scholar's appetite for primary performance evidence could be supported by a more expansive practical and technical vocabulary with which to discuss it.

Between 2011 and 2017 I interviewed actors, directors and designers of Shakespeare working for and at some of the major producing institutions in the United States and the United Kingdom. Being based at the Shakespeare Institute in Stratford upon Avon for some of this time was fortunate for me, as I had access to key RSC staff members as well as actors who performed on those famous stages. In London, I was able to make use of some longstanding contacts I have with actors and directors connected with Shakespeare's Globe, where I served as head of research from 1999 to 2002. The American respondents in this volume have connections with the Guthrie Theater in Minneapolis, the flagship regional theatre in the United States, and the institution where I began my career as an assistant director, and with the American Shakespeare Center, where I directed and taught on their partnership MFA programme (with Mary Baldwin University) in Shakespeare and Performance.

The interviews vary in type, tone and length: most were conducted face to face, in cafés, bars, pubs, green rooms, canteens, theatre lobbies or dressing rooms. These were largely informal, lively conversations, which very quickly departed from the prepared list of questions I took to each interview as backup. Some were conducted in the Royal Shakespeare Company's administrative offices in Stratford upon Avon, or in the quiet calm of the Shakespeare Institute, just around the corner. Some respondents invited me into their homes, to share insights over tea and biscuits, one took place on the piazza outside the Globe, in between matinee and evening performances. Where face-to-face meetings were not possible, I used Skype connections and a series of telephone and email exchanges to connect with the respondents. Once completed, the interviews were transcribed in full and then edited. The edited interviews were then sent to the respondents for approval, either directly or via their agents. Elsewhere, I have been lucky in reaching some far-flung respondents through the good offices of people I have never met, people working in busy London theatres, who took time out of their day to locate an actor I was unable to, and forward them an interview transcript for approval. Tamara Moore of the Young Vic is one such person, and to her I owe a debt of thanks.

When the respondents were asked to review their interview transcriptions I promised that these would be reprinted in their entirety, so as to capture the individual voices recorded here and the flow of ideas that is unique to each respondent. Another reason the interviews appear in full is to allow individual readers to use the interviews for research guided by their own interests and agendas. There are already plenty of great books which will tell you what their authors think about the work of a Shakespearean actor, director, designer or coach. I want this book to be the conduit for an altogether more direct conversation between reader and respondent. That said, the volume concludes with a brief consideration of the 'patterns in the wallpaper' (as I see them) linking the practices espoused by the various respondents across job descriptions and disciplines.

The respondents

Many of the people interviewed are old friends of mine, others I regard as mentors. Of those people I met for the first time at our interview, I would say most would now fit into one of the categories above. For this reason, I choose to dispense with the convention of using surnames-only to identify them.

In her interview, the actor **Emily Taaffe** notes: 'When I read a play just for pleasure, I read it "as a whole": reading a play for work is reading from a character's point of view, which is a very different thing' (p. 82). I want to begin with this deceptively straightforward distinction, because it summarizes the difference between the way a general reader might read a play ('as a whole') and the way an actor works with a text ('from a character's point of view'). Actor **Jonathan McGuinness** regards '[T]he time before rehearsals begin as an opportunity to keep reminding myself of the scope and sense of the whole play, and what that story is' as '[o]nce you begin to rehearse, you start to focus on your own character and your own scenes; this is what most of the work is about for you, when you're in a rehearsal room' (p. 61). **Jade Anouka** goes further in emphasizing this common practice of reading the text from a character's specific perspective, and confesses, 'I don't think I've *ever* read a Shakespeare play without (unintentionally) casting myself! I'm always reading the play from someone's point of view' (p. 21; emphasis in the original). This is probably because of the continuing influence – some would say dominance – of Stanislavski's system, in modern actor training. Emily's favourite drama school anecdote playfully echoes this sentiment: 'There's that joke about this ... when you do *The Cherry Orchard*, people might ask: "What's it about?" and you say: "It's about this maid called Dunyasha ..." because you always view the play solely through your character's eyes' (pp. 82–3). While I hope to avoid as many casual generalities and binaries as I can, it is fair to say that if an actor considers their specific character or role as their primary responsibility, it will follow that responsibility for a production's overall narrative and aesthetic falls more to the director and creative team.

The actor **Jonathan Slinger** describes a kind of Stanislavskian historicism in his approach, which allows the character's 'biography' (historically or imaginatively sourced) to inform characterization as much as the historically and culturally specific meanings of words which seem deceptively familiar to modern actors and readers. Readers with an interest in the ongoing debates about Shakespeare's text and subtexts will be drawn to Jonathan's discussion of the ongoing 'internal dialogue' (p. 79) between what is spoken by the actor and what the character is thinking; this in many respects distils an ongoing dialogue between Shakespeare's early modern texts and twentieth- or twenty-first-century modern theatre practice.

Actor **Juliet Rylance**'s interview describes the elements of her Stanislavski-based RADA training which continue to contribute to her approach to rehearsals. For Juliet, this is only part of being 'in play' with a Shakespeare text; a responsive ear and voice must also remain 'in play' with the rhythms and resonances of Shakespeare's language (pp. 74–5). Actor **Pippa Nixon** agrees that 'when you breathe properly your voice drops into its natural resonance, and it is not constricted … and that enables you to articulate the language' (p. 70) and wonders 'whether, if you abandon yourself to the text, and have the technique behind you and start to inhabit the text … that it might start changing you … working on you, transforming you' (p. 70). For Juliet and Pippa, the psycho-physical basis of Stanislavski's system seems to complement, not to compete, with a more technical approach to verse speaking. It is a question of balance, as Pippa notes, in words that are echoed by many of the actors in this volume: 'once you know the mechanics of it … then you can start playing … I hope that I am getting better, technically, at working with the verse, but I don't want to be strictly obedient to the technicality of the verse, at the expense of investing in the character' (p. 68).

This is not to suggest that the balance is easy to strike, or that Stanislavski and Shakespeare enjoy an uncontroversial relationship at all times. I was struck by the conviction with which actor **Amer Hlehel** spoke of Stanislavski's system. Amer describes his job as finding a way to play very specific actions, so that the 'emotion' as such can emerge as a by-product of the action.

> Stanislavski explained that you need to see things – don't feel, see. If you see things, your body will feel, and your senses will respond naturally. You can't decide for the character 'Oh, I'm sad now,' because sadness is a result, and not the fabric of our experience and reaction to things, you need the process on stage to get to the result. I try to ask myself in every line: 'What is my action?' So, when I say: 'The isle is full of noises, / Sounds and sweet airs that give delight and

hurt not' (*The Tempest*, 3.2.135–6), what am I saying in that line? What's my action? I'm saying two things in that line; I'm saying to Trinculo and Stephano: 'Don't worry', and also saying, 'I am in love with this place', So if I do both the result will be like a hunger, like I 'miss' something. So, it's about that by the end. If there is no action then the line means only that this place is pretty. There is no goal in it. (p. 49)

The director **Greg Doran** espouses a rhetoric-first approach to characterization: '[t]he point of the process is to start off by getting actors to see … how powerful the tools of rhetoric are, and then to get them to understand that they need to look for the clues that are in the text, before they try and work out who their character is' (p. 121). **Eve Best** agrees that one should 'pay attention to the verse because there's so much information in it. You are being directed very clearly, by the greatest writer of all time, how to say something, so it seems sensible to listen to his instructions' (p. 29). **Alex Hassell** also argues that the more an actor can invest in the technical elements of the language, the less they need to do in other areas.

[I]t would be better not think about 'character' at all, when you're looking at the text, so then you can see more clearly that the text is riddled with inconsistencies and contradictions, just as any interesting human being is. If you begin by thinking 'Oh, what's my character like?' you then iron out all of these amazing inconsistencies: having the strength to *not* decide what sort of character you are and thereby limit it, and to search for as many inconsistencies and contradictions as you can, is an immensely important thing. (pp. 44–5; emphasis in the original)

Alex's approach owes much to his collaboration with his colleague at The Factory, director **Tim Carroll**, who describes himself as increasingly 'fascistic' (p. 104) in his approach to verse speaking. Tim admits to a fascination with what is difficult, and professes a suspicion of editorial adjustments to the text. He also eschews directorial tricks and technical sleights of hand, preferring to put his faith in the verse and the actors' facility with it. This trust is shared by the director **Mike Alfreds**, whose practice has influenced Tim's and that of many other respondents in this volume, as well as my own. I have observed Mike's work in rehearsals for two productions at Shakespeare's Globe, and it is fair to say that he is justly renowned for his rigour. His contribution to this volume reads less like an interview, and more like a masterclass in acting, which sets out Mike's views on verse speaking, and identifies many common pitfalls he believes the actor must avoid when working with a Shakespeare text. Mike warns that '[w]orking on Shakespeare requires immense rigour. Only through discipline can actors achieve any creative freedom. Approximation and generalization are deadly. Accuracy and specificity lead to life. It is there within these texts, waiting to be released' (p. 101). Rigour is second nature to the actor and dancer **Ankur Bahl**, who places a high value on daily training; he notes with regret that, unlike dancers or musicians, most actors do not tend to regard daily training as a prerequisite for performance. In comparison to dance, no similar relationship between professional work and ongoing training is similarly enshrined in the context of the acting 'industry'. Likewise Tim Carroll describes how at The Factory actors do not rehearse so much as 'train to be good at doing verse, to be good at responding to each other's offers. We train to have strong voices, to have good spatial awareness, to be physically fit and flexible' (p. 107).

Another Factory alumnus, the actor **Colin Hurley** describes how his parallel career as a teacher in drama schools has, as he puts it, 'completed the circle for me. There have been days, when I have been teaching in the day, performing in the evening, when I'd remember what I had asked of my students, and would have to raise my own game, and practice what I had been preaching. If you want to really learn about something, teach it' (p. 53). Actor **Andrew Long** also identifies important points of contact between his experience of training (in particular his movement training), teaching and performing. Actor and director **Yolanda Vazquez** notes that she still uses 'pretty much everything I learnt in training' (p. 88) at the Drama Centre, and her interview unpacks these constituent elements from her dual perspectives of actor and director. Their interviews specifically and (I hope) this book more generally suggest that theatre practice evolves in a gradual fashion, with tried and tested methodologies being used to respond to a wide range of rehearsal, teaching and performance contexts.

Not everyone in this volume is a product of a drama school training, and for **Geraldine Collinge**, working with Shakespeare is all about 'change' (p. 111); her role as director of events at the RSC entails a 'process of breaking down traditional barriers, bringing people closer to Shakespeare, changing people's perceptions of Shakespeare and changing their relationship to Shakespeare' (p. 112). The actor **T. R. Knight** goes further, openly acknowledging the politics of access Geraldine refers to: 'Shakespeare is for everyone, to be spoken by everyone, no matter your education or dialect. I strongly believe that gender should not dictate casting, and anything that smacks of stale "tradition" should be upended' (p. 56). The director **Renato Rocha** questions assumptions about Shakespeare's universal appeal. Citing his experience in educational and social projects in Brazil's favelas, he says, 'The first step is always identifying how this story is still relevant nowadays – what it does to us now, and what its relationship to contemporary society is' (p. 156). Director **Polly Findlay** begins from a similar starting point, by asking herself, '[W]hat was the gesture of this play – what was the social function of the play – at the time in which it was written, and how can I best replicate that in a contemporary context?' (p. 126).

Director **Ethan McSweeny** is brave enough to tackle the thorny issue of the director's 'concept', in a frank and clear-sighted interview in which he maintains 'the reason concept gets a bad name, is that there are some directors who do things *to* plays, and that's not very nice. However, there is a big difference between doing something *to* a play and doing something *with* a play and I think we are obligated to the latter' (p. 139; emphases in the original). Ethan goes on to follow Ralph Berry in identifying four basic concept models, which may be used to make connections and comparisons between a wide range of twentieth- and twenty-first-century Shakespeare productions on both sides of the Atlantic. Designers **Tom Piper** and **Bunny Christie** recognize similar distinctions. Tom admits that 'the big decision is the whole issue of period, that is, where we are going to set it, and when' (p. 150) while Bunny emphasizes the same historicism in needing to know 'what era we want to set the play in' (p. 109). Once this has been established, Tom argues that 'design is actually a sort of sculptural medium that happens over time. The design fulfils its purpose based on the way the actors change it. The costumes, the stories, the use of light: these are the things that occupy the design over time and make it work' (p. 149). For this, of course, it is essential to have a detailed understanding of 'what the action of the scene is' (p. 109), as Bunny puts it.

Music is included in the wider discussion of production design, and **Claire van Kampen** and **Bruce O'Neil** offer different and surprising perspectives on the composition and integration of music for Shakespeare's plays. Bruce's interest in the way in which music appeals to what he calls the 'lizard brain' (pp. 145–6) suggests that music's potential for meaning-making in the theatre remains largely untapped. Claire cites her extensive experience composing for early modern instruments in the Globe space as career-changing; she argues against what she views as the cinematic practice of underscoring, asking composers and directors to follow textual clues more closely when integrating sound and spoken text (pp. 161–6). In different ways, both Bruce and Claire ask us to reconsider the action of music in Shakespeare's plays.

I wish I had been able to give more consideration to the role of coaches at the larger Shakespeare-producing theatres; coaches in voice and movement may not feature prominently in critical reviews of productions, but their work is crucial to any production. At institutions such as the Globe, the RSC, the Shakespeare Theatre and the large Shakespeare festivals in the United States, voice and movement coaches will be responsible not just for maintaining the vocal and physical health of the actors over the course of the season, but arguably they are the most invested stakeholders in what some would identify as a 'house style' of performance. **Michael Corbidge** notes that '[o]nce the show is underway directors will leave, movement directors leave, technical designers leave, the creative team leaves – so then it's up to people like me to maintain the integrity of the show' (p. 116). Michael also describes working with individual actors in a kind of bespoke diagnostic process, listening carefully to assess quickly the areas in which he can support the actor's vocal development. As a movement coach at Shakespeare's Globe for many years, **Sian Williams** has contributed hugely to successive companies' understanding of the space and how to play in it. She clearly relishes the chance to choreograph Globe jigs with actors, rather than dancers, and sees dance in this context as 'a gift that welcomes and inspires the audience, hopefully making them feel as though they could (almost) get up and join in' (p. 172).

Sian also cites the influence of devised work (with her company The Kosh) in shaping her regular work with Shakespeare, a sensibility she shares with the actor **Sandy Grierson**; Sian relishes physical devised work 'that can refresh and nourish this "regular" work by giving you insights into the different ways people respond to information and new stories' (p. 173) whereas Sandy describes how Tadeusz Kantor's practice of generating and then rejecting devised ideas 'is more to do with a state of mind … [a]s an actor you're a kind of ghost' (p. 32); devising methodologies similarly produce narratives and 'ghosts of these unused ideas' (p. 33) as part of a process that is infused with 'a very important sense of memory' (p. 32).

Sian's view of performance as 'a gift' (p. 172), and Sandy's acknowledgement of 'ghosts' (p. 33) are both echoed by the dancer, actor, teacher and mime artist, Lindsay Kemp, my friend and mentor, who died on 24 August 2018. I was inspired by Lindsay's unflinching and lifelong commitment to 'lifting the spirits of the public' (p. 135), and his interview traces his engagement with Shakespeare back to his childhood memories of dancing and 'entertaining the neighbours, their children and dogs in our communal air-raid shelter, as the bombs were dropping' (pp. 130–1), as well as to his career-defining work *Flowers: A Pantomime for Jean Genet.* Every performance Lindsay gave or directed was 'all for the audience's' pleasure. Acting involves taking risks, playing dangerously … this brings the essential element of excitement to the theatre. Risk is an essential part of performance, even though it can have disastrous results, sometimes! My tradition, my roots tell me that you've got to thrill an audience, walking the tightrope where they sense you could fall (p. 133). Described in this way, it is tempting to regard this element of risk as the exclusive domain of the performer, but the experience of trying to write this book persuades me otherwise: the actor, director, artist, author and scholar share an obligation to face the public and own their choices, sooner or later, and it is perhaps only the preparation processes and opportunities for revision which differ, when all is said and done. With this daunting prospect in mind, I would like to give the last (wise) words of this introduction to my good friend, the actor **John Harrell**, whose career at the American Shakespeare Center and elsewhere has given him the opportunity to work on every one of Shakespeare's plays. He puts it far better than I can: 'I know nothing about Shakespeare. I think it's important to reassert that every now and then, because humility in the face of such an artistic totality is indispensable. What I believe about Shakespeare is always subject to revision. His plays continue to confound us all, which is why we continue to produce and to write about him' (pp. 39–40).

The Interviews

Cast

JADE ANOUKA, ACTOR

Text work

I begin by getting to know the play purely from my character's point of view: first I read the scenes that my character is in, to get a sense of the character and their story. Then I look at how my character relates to other characters, what I say to and about others and then work out who *those* people are. I very much read the play from my own character's perspective. In all honesty, I don't think I've *ever* read a Shakespeare play without (unintentionally) casting myself! I'm always reading the play from someone's point of view.

Every director works very differently. I was very lucky to be cast by Tim Carroll in *The Merchant of Venice* at the RSC soon after drama school, and from him I learned a great exercise when speaking blank verse: the company were given a ball, to be held by whoever was speaking at the time in a given scene. As the speaker reached the last stressed syllable of their last verse line, they had to throw the ball up in the air; whoever spoke next had to either snatch it out of the air or catch it on the first stressed syllable of their first verse line. This exercise helps you to make sure your energy at the end of a line goes up, rather than dropping off the vocal energy at the end, which often happens. And, instead of becoming intimidated by the rules of speaking iambic pentameter, this exercise really showed me that, in fact, line endings were my friend! It was probably Tim who encouraged me to learn the rhythm of iambic pentameter as a kind of base rhythm, so you know it's there, and from that point on to treat the verse more like jazz, so that you don't sound robotic or repetitive, and (hopefully) you can improvise, you can 'sing' on top of that supporting rhythm.

Actioning the text

I've been working more recently with Phyllida [Lloyd], who is really big on actioning the text. She asks us to identify a specific action for each thought, using the punctuation marks in the text to help define the length of each thought. You are identifying exactly what you are trying to do to your scene partner with each particular thought. I work much better with image-based actions, ones which I can picture physically, for example, 'to crown someone' or 'to hug someone'.

Shakespeare's poetic language is potentially a bit overwhelming, and I find the most useful approach for me is to take these very big, rich ideas and to try to boil them down to the simplest, strongest action I can, even to the point of physicalizing the action with a gesture. That can help keep you focused on what you are trying to *do* to the other person … your character is *saying* all of this, but it helps to ask: 'what am I actually trying to *achieve*?'

Actioning the text is really helpful for those bits of text that I might struggle with, so it is something I do even when I'm not working with someone like Phyllida who works that way. In fact, the two approaches I've just described are both really helpful. If I don't understand something, first I will go back to iambic pentameter, because finding out which words are stressed will help me to better understand the meaning of the line. If I'm not sure what to *play* on a line, I'll make sure that I give it a strong action first: choosing a strong action will tell you quickly whether you're generally in the right area, or not.

Phyllida likes us to mark in the actions in our text before rehearsals begin, because that way actors come in with very clear choices. Then, as you start working with your scene partner, you realize that some of your choices don't work, because they don't connect to those of your scene partner. But that forces you to adapt, and to make another strong choice, so because you weren't allowed to come in with any lines that you are 'just saying' ... those lines don't exist!

Playing male roles

Playing Hotspur was a big thing for me. He's quite a 'bloke', a warrior, full of bravado, he's full of these traits that, as a woman, you hardly ever get to play, especially not in a Shakespeare play! A lot of Shakespeare's female characters are either domestic or romantic, so, being able to take up space physically, and take up space with your words ... I'm sure that was helpful in all sorts of ways. Getting a chance to *not apologize* ... it was nice to be on stage and only have 'my' story to worry about; for my story to be a story in its own right, not just one in relation to a man's story ... in relation to someone else's story ... that was great!

Playing Mark Antony, you have to *not* think about Marlon Brando, and all the other famous actors who've played the role! That tradition carries so much weight, you have to let it go, and strip it all back to: *what* am I saying? *why* am I saying it? *who* am I talking to? *how* do I want to change them with this line? Then, when you add in more detail by actioning the text, it all makes sense. It's also how we get so much variety: it is so interesting to see different people play the same part, because they will have chosen such different actions. You can't play a role the same way as anyone else, because even though your objectives may be the same as another actor in the same role, you will have chosen different actions on the way to pursue those objectives. So that's why each performance is unique.

ANKUR BAHL, ACTOR/DANCER

Auditions

I trained and worked as a dancer, and had never performed Shakespeare before my RSC audition in the autumn of 2011.

The call to audition was for actors with strong physical abilities and so the first audition was to test movement – no text. I went along and was in my comfort zone, responding to physical tasks among other dancers. The real challenge began when I was called back for a second round of auditions and was asked to prepare speeches from two roles that I would understudy in the upcoming rep of *Twelfth Night*, *The Tempest* and *The Comedy of Errors*.

My prior experience of Shakespeare was my high-school English class; I had very little idea how to work with verse and was pretty sure reciting 'dee-dum, dee-dum, dee-dum' to myself wasn't going to land me the job. So, I called all my experienced actor friends who had worked with Shakespeare, and set up one-to-one working sessions with them. In those conversations, a couple pieces of advice really resonated with me:

1. If you don't understand it, you'll never be able to play it.
2. Shakespearean verse might feel like a challenge, but playing the text should not start as a technical exercise – start with an honest investigation of the human emotions and relationships of the play.
3. Trust your ability as a physical storyteller.

So I started by demystifying the text; going word for word, 'What does this mean? What is this a metaphor for? What is this a reference to?' I read all the notes in the various editions that I had, and tested my understanding by explaining the text to friends in laymen's terms: 'This means I love you this much' or 'This means I just want to shag you'. This understanding of the text enabled me to think about the characters in a deep, heartfelt way.

Once I'd got the text under my belt and really understood how I wanted to play it, another revelation came when actor Shiv Grewal recommended I rehearse the speeches outdoors. Having to produce the sound and play the character against the elements allowed me to be less inhibited about my physicality, got my lungs and voice working in a fully embodied way and gave me confidence and enjoyment with the text for the first time.

A dancer's approach to Shakespeare

A dancer's life is extremely regimented and disciplined; a dancer starts every day of his or her working life with an hour to an hour and a half of training. Whether that's a ballet class, a yoga class, any sort of technique – you're in class every day and you're constantly fine-tuning your craft.

Being in rep at the RSC proved the perfect place to apply a dancer's approach to continuous development. Vocal coaches, accent coaches, people who wanted to talk about rhetoric, people who wanted to look at the text and break it down, other actors who had done it tons of times before and were more than willing to help, all formed a catalogue of resources available to learn and develop as an actor, a performer and a Shakespearean.

To be a Shakespearean actor (to be any kind of actor, I would argue) you have to be aware of your physicality. The notion of being on breath and being front-footed were skills that I had developed as a performer at DV8 physical theatre, skills that have proved incredibly important at the RSC. Head of Movement Struan Leslie and Michael Corbidge from the Voice Department have encouraged me to tap in to that knowledge, saying, 'Okay you know how to use your body, you know how to be on breath, you know how to initiate movement and breath and voice at the same time; now let's apply that to what we're doing with the verse.' This has allowed me to approach working on Shakespeare in my own way; perhaps starting from a more physical place than other actors, but in the end, heading to the same goal as everyone else in the company: a performance that resonates with the audience.

Physical approaches to text

The language in Shakespeare's plays is very muscular and physical in its use of verbs and action. Furthermore, each character comes with his or her own ticks and nuances that can be brought to bear in the body of the performer. For example, the way Andrew Aguecheek holds himself and uses his limbs (I imagine them to be extremely lanky) is completely different to the assuredness of Ferdinand, even when he finds himself in an unknown land after a shipwreck. In rehearsing the Dromios, I found it exciting to play with different physical approaches. Sometimes it was mimicry, doing exactly what the text or the stage directions indicate. Sometimes (and more interestingly) I chose a concrete physicality to either contradict or highlight what the audience was hearing against what they were seeing, abstracting the physical and textual connections to add to the confusion of the situation.

As trained bodies, we dancers are very aware of every little movement we make. This can be a really powerful tool. At DV8, Lloyd Newson spoke a lot about audiences watching a piece of dance and thinking, 'I can't do that' but hearing text and thinking, 'I can do that', because we all speak. In working with Shakespeare, I have found the opposite can be true. Oftentimes an audience member will feel: 'I may or may not understand that text, I most certainly wouldn't speak that way in my day-to-day life, however, when I see that person move like that I know that person, I've seen that'. So, the physicality that the characters inhabit is often the most immediately tangible aspect of a Shakespeare play for an audience member. If you as an actor can tap into that physicality knowingly, then you can give audiences something they can immediately latch on to, which can help them find their way into the beauty of the text.

Language

In dance, if you've done – for lack of a better example – your *tendus* and your *pliés* in the morning, when you get on stage you can perform the choreography to its fullest without worrying about your knees bending or your feet pointing, because you know they will. Working Shakespeare's text has proven to be similar. If I've worked the muscularity of the text, the line endings, the punctuation, if I've really thought about the pronouns and worked the verbs in the learning and the rehearsing and the thinking about the text, then when I come to perform it, I don't have to hit the audience over the head with all of that. I can trust that work has embedded itself, and can just come out and tell the story, which makes being a dancer and a Shakespearean actor very similar.

EVE BEST, ACTOR

The initial work I do on a project varies from play to play. For a Chekhov play I might do a lot of detailed background work. For Shakespeare I would work on the words. For Harold Pinter's *The Homecoming*, I did no background work at all.

My character, Ruth, had hardly anything to say – everything that goes on with her is in the realms of the physical and the instinctual. It felt right not to have done work with my head before I arrived at rehearsals so that I could keep my instincts clear.

In my second year at Oxford University, Ian McKellen was the resident professor of drama and I was in his group of students while he worked with us on *Uncle Vanya*. The system he taught us was a technique Mike Alfreds uses, of going through the text several times, asking different questions and making a list of direct quotations from the play that answer each question. These include: What does my character say about herself? What do I say about each of the other characters? What do the other characters say about me? What do I say about the world? What do I say about the weather? By the time you have done that work you've gone through the play several times and you are not only very familiar with it, you've also been very precise. You haven't made anything up or made any assumptions about a character before you start exploring it. It's an almost forensic approach that I find very useful and have used often ever since.

Learning Shakespeare

Learning Shakespeare is just like learning French or any other language. When you're fluent in a language it is in your body, your blood and your bones. You're not using your brain to speak the words – they're an extension of your body. I've found the most useful thing to do as soon as possible is to get the words into my body. I want to be so familiar with them that they are not frightening or foreign, they're part of me and I'm used to saying them. Before rehearsals start I'll go for walks with the script in my pocket, stomping up country lanes saying the words out loud, getting them into my body.

Working on verse

When you're working on verse, there are often gifts that you can get through just being very specific with the text and understanding what it's telling you. Opinions vary widely on the best way to approach Shakespeare … and of course, each to his own. I like to pay attention to the verse because there's so much information in it. You are being directed very clearly, by the greatest writer of all time, how to say something, so it seems sensible to listen to his instructions. The mind of a genius is showing us where he wants emphasis, and where sense comes, and where breath comes. The text guides us to speak in an incredibly natural way; and following it, driving through to the ends of lines, paying attention to the iambic pentameter and breathing at the ends of lines, you find something that often sounds as if it had been written yesterday.

I was once doing an exercise on Hamlet's 'To be or not to be' soliloquy (*Hamlet,* 3.1.55–87). We discovered that everyone wanted to pause, naturalistically, in the middle of the line:

'And by opposing end them; to die: to sleep –' (59)

so that the line would be:

'And by opposing end them (PAUSE …) to die: to sleep –'

But something about introducing that pause midline made it less exciting. It made it safe. It gave everyone – the character, the actor, the audience – time to think, it was literally a breathing space, and the speech became somehow measured and analytical. However, driving the line on, as it seems Shakespeare is instructing us to do – because it is all one line – this thought comes at you like a tidal wave. It's exhilarating and much more interesting to hear and to experience. It's more raw, more unexpected, more visceral. Instead of reasoned logic, it has the blurted energy of a young man in crisis, with thoughts tumbling out of his mouth, grappling to find sense in his fractured world. It's jagged, not measured, much more like real speech and real life.

SANDY GRIERSON, ACTOR

Preparation

How you begin your process depends, I think, on where you are in life at that point. Sometimes you are out of work and you have all the time in the world to prepare. Sometimes you have to be careful not to over-prepare. Sometimes the longer you have on that personal relationship with the text, the more rigid your reading becomes, the more it is then going to be painful when it is broken, which it inevitably will be. You have to be flexible when you get in that room, depending on who else is in there with you, who is in the scene with you, what the director's vision is.

Text

I like to jump in styles of learning lines, to go from the right scansion and see how it sounds, and then do it with the thoughts, reading for the line of thought ... whether you are just reading to the line ending, or with length of thought, going all the way through lines. Then, jam on the rhythms, and see how they sound without any thought to scansion or poetry in mind. Again, there is no point in doing it all at once; it's dependent on how long your rehearsal period is. The one thing that's a killer is getting stuck on something and just doing it the same way over and over again. Ultimately with a show you will end up falling into a pattern but for my benefit I'd rather be doing it a little bit off-kilter at the beginning and find my way there through a process, than to walk in and think, 'That's how I would do it – this is my delivery and this is what I need to do.'

What I really like to do is read it as a complete script first; I find the more creative ideas to begin with. Even if my ideas are nowhere near where the director is thinking of taking it, I just have a sort of gist of what I think the play is sort of about – how I think my characters relate to that idea and how those ideas or those themes affect my character. So in that sense, I can establish what my function is ... what the overall gist is, as I perceive it.

A lot of actors begin before rehearsals with their character work: lists, circumstances, questions. I tend to think that that's work I do in the rehearsal rooms. In the early stages, I try and read the play more generally – I like to be surprised when rehearsals begin. I like to put myself in the position of having to listen really carefully to the other scenes and listen closely to the other actors, so it's not just a case of listening out for a cue line.

In terms of line-learning at the start of a process, I can't just sit and read a script and learn lines like that. I also don't really learn them very effectively if I just talk them like I'm talking now – I need to sort of project and I almost need to annunciate them really, really clearly so that muscle memory starts to work; otherwise I can get lost very easily.

Kantor and physical approaches to Shakespeare

Aside from text work, there is a sense of physical life in each and every character. When I played Ariel, David Farr was talking about the production being inspired by Tadeusz Kantor, the Polish director. My mother took me to see a Kantor when I was 12 – the last show – *Today's My Birthday*. He died when he was making it. My mother had seen *The Dead Class* at Edinburgh Art College and was absolutely blown away by it. It blew me away too. I was bored to tears by theatre and then I went to this weird spectacle and ... It's the only time I'd ever stood in a theatre – I think I was the first person to stand up – it wasn't like I knew that that was what you were meant to do, it was just this thing happening. I was totally blown away by it, and that took me down a certain route in theatre. One of Kantor's actresses called Zofia Kalinska came to Edinburgh and did a one-woman show in a basement in Demarco's space. I went to see that and had much the same experience. It was about her life relating to classic female characters – Medea, Salome – it blew me away again. She is a phenomenal performer, and so I hung around and there were a few other people that hung around and she said she'd do a workshop. So I stayed in touch, and she did a show the next year and I had a little part in that. The year after that she did a show called *A Little Requiem for Kantor*, which I was in and played Kantor as a boy. It then toured around Europe and then to Brazil and it was amazing and all that time I was training with her and going to Krakow with her.

Later, when I was offered Ariel, one of the first people I looked at was Jan Kott. I find what he writes about Shakespeare provokes really interesting ideas. You just get a sense that he's enjoying it as food and wine as opposed to anything too dry. So when I was cast in *The Tempest*, I read some of his work discussing it. He talks about Ariel as being this sort of slow-moving youth and I did think immediately of Kantor and playing that part of the little boy and I kind of agree: The more you try and run about as a sprite character I think the more obvious your humanness appears. For me Kantor is more to do with a state of mind. As an actor you're a kind of ghost. There's a very important sense of memory which I think works really well with *The Tempest* because everything in that play is memory: 'do you remember this, do you remember that' 'you don't remember but I remember' – the whole thing is about the possession of history.

The process of devising work

I think the other useful tool for doing Shakespeare in my experience with Zofia is the importance of devised work. You create a lot of material, especially in the first few weeks – more and more material and you're not even sure which direction you're going in – and then you gradually find something and then you sit on that and then you create more material and at the end of every day 99 per cent of what you've done is just gone – you'll never really touch on it again. But the fact that it happened means that you're onto the next thing which leads you onto the next thing which leads you on to the next thing and so forth. I think sometimes the ghosts of these unused ideas can make the background a bit richer or just silently underpin ... even if it's just in the confidence of the actor who knows that they have worked towards one idea and chosen another. This said, the audience shouldn't come away from it thinking 'that must have been an interesting process' ... that is not what we are trying to achieve!

I suppose the hope is that your training sits in and you don't wear it on your surface. It should be in your bone marrow and then you forget about it. When something works in the rehearsal room the first time and then you rework it and rework it and rework it – invariably it changes as you look at it – you know what is coming. If you improvise something comedic, of course the first time that you do it everyone in the room falls about – the actors are finding it hard to carry on. It's this wonderful thing and you feel that you've found something, and then the next time you come back to it, it's about knowing what it was that worked, and knowing that it works, but it won't work necessarily for *you* again. The first time that you get this idea in front of an audience, hopefully the ghost of that original thing comes into the room. If not, then you realize that you've made a dire mistake and that it was just the giddy Friday afternoon session and it should never have stayed in the show in the first place. The audience can reteach you your immediate response to something which came through the rehearsal process that you completely forgot.

Instincts

As important as it is to have a process that works for you, it's equally important to follow your impulses. You have to know where they come from and how to respond to them. My gut instincts tend to work in a spatial sense, when something physically isn't right, I become aware. I can recognize when I feel like I'm in the wrong place physically on stage or in the wrong physical dynamic between me and somebody else. That is an instinct I tend to trust. I know when it's right for me that the words have a sort of physical impact. When this happens, then I feel like I can begin to trust my instincts. Of course, I am interested in lines, but they tend to have more abstract ideas about stuff as opposed to a gut feeling. I don't tend to get a gut feeling from text – when it manifests itself physically, be that in the mouth or in the body then I can start to feel the impulses and read if they feel right or if I feel wrong. I don't think that the page has ever been my strongest access point.

I'm not a massive football fan but I do think it ends up as quite a good metaphor for a process like this, because you're in your position and you're ready in your position and you know what your position is. You know what you're meant to be doing and knowing who's supporting you, behind you and all the way back and who you're meant to be passing forward to, whose job it is to stick the ball in the back of the net, when you're allowed a pop yourself and all of that stuff. If you know all of that, then it gives you a lot of support within which to improvise, within which to play and to play to make the right choices for the story you're telling, knowing the range within which you can play. You shouldn't be going into a performance looking for something massive; I've been there with devising shows and it's never pleasant. If there's a scene that I'm not sure about, I want to be getting myself into a position so that I feel that I'm not going to have to go and change everything after a few performances. I mean they're not going to change the lighting plan for me after the tech, there's not going to be change just because you want to go somewhere else. The feeling itself can shift all the time and how you're playing off each other will change day by day and season by season, but you can't change things that are adversely going to affect the clarity of the story.

The influence of training

I suppose the question of process is always going to be heavily affected by whatever training you've had or professional experiences you've learnt from. I think that's why the physical approach resonates with me, sometimes ahead of the text. As I mentioned before, my basic training was with Zofia Kalinska, but I also trained with another teacher called David Johnstone in Edinburgh. David's background is mime but he also trained with another Polish actor called Ossetynski. I don't know how to describe his approach – he's sort of Michael Chekhovian – he kind of had a link with Grotowski. Zofia and David were my mentors and they still are – I'm in touch with them – it's very much just the two of them that were really important. Their knowledge and experience of physical storytelling has become a central part of my process.

While David did lab with Ossetynski, he worked in an outdoor theatre on the outskirts of Los Angeles, and every summer they would do Shakespeare. He would do a lot of speeches with me when I was training, but professionally I'd only ever done a production of *Romeo and Juliet* in Scotland before getting the job at the RSC. It was a weird one actually. Basically, the actors playing Romeo and Juliet were brought in for a week's work on text, but by the end of that week they'd got rid of Romeo. The guy playing Mercutio was bumped up to Romeo and I was bumped up from the Prince to Mercutio. It was quite a weird sort of atmosphere but there were a lot of lively performers and some good storytelling.

The RST, then and now

I remember seeing *Troilus and Cressida* here years ago. I found it really inaccessible and miles away. It feels so much more intimate in the Royal Shakespeare Theatre now. It's hard to believe that there's a thousand people out there. There's not really one big soliloquy to the audience for me – Ariel has a couple of wee moments with the audience but there's no sustained conversation/eye contact. But whenever I do look up and around it's clear that the audience are in the room with us, and we're very much experiencing something together.

JOHN HARRELL, ACTOR

Text work

At one time, I'd have said that the first thing I do is to read the play, but I've now been in many of these plays so many times that I no longer do this. Now, I take a stack of blank notecards and start copying my cues on one side and my lines on the other. I find this exercise much more useful than simply sitting and reading the scenes that I am in. If my text is in verse, I copy it verse line by verse line, counting beats and considering anomalies as I go. I also take the opportunity, after writing out each line, to consult footnotes and dictionaries and such to make sure that I understand each bit. I'm talking here about achieving a semantic and syntactic understanding of the text, not necessarily a literary one. This pass through the script is not the time for me to decide what kind of character I'm playing or whether his values reflect my own. It is merely a chance for me to clarify what I am saying, and to determine whether any of it sounds funny.

I'm pleased to say that, now that I've been at this Shakespeare game for a while, his language only rarely seems obscure to me. Over time, the alienating power of the thees and the thous, the withals and the wherefores seems to fall away, and the sense of the text is no longer mysterious. I have to remind myself, though, that audiences have mostly not broken through the cognitive barrier that keeps early modern English so distant. One of the challenges, then, is trying to calibrate line readings so that they carry the emotional weight and dramatic intention that the play requires without sacrificing plain clarity. I genuinely believe that most of Shakespeare's lines can be said in such a way that any audience member who is not actively resisting the performance can follow along, without an actor's having to resort to indicative gesture and blunt-force emoting. As I've heard Ralph Cohen say, if you followed a conversation in French as well as you can follow a clearly performed Shakespeare monologue, you'd feel as if you understood French.

The opportunities afforded by Shakespeare's language are many. Much of the time, his text is just a pleasure to say out loud. Even seeming clunkers such as Claudio's 'Are our eyes our own?' (*Much Ado About Nothing*, 4.1.71) reveal a suppleness when one applies one's voice patiently. And the joy of reciting Oberon's 'I know a bank where the wild thyme blows' speech (*A Midsummer Night's Dream*, 2.1.249–67) borders on self-ravishment.

I have long believed that Shakespeare is underappreciated as a comic playwright. I'll grant that the horn jokes are often tedious, and the man can get bogged down in quillets of the law, but few human achievements are as sublime as Dogberry's 'God save the foundation!' (*Much Ado About Nothing*, 5.1.307) or Andrew Aguecheek's 'I have't in my nose, too' (*Twelfth Night*, 2.3.158).

Rehearsal process

As I've already mentioned, I start with the note cards. This not only affords me an opportunity to consider the sinew of the text in small detail, it also begins the long and perhaps never-quite-finished process of memorization. Next comes rehearsal. This process generally begins with a read-through, followed by a fairly open discussion of the text, what it means and what some performative possibilities may be. At least in the American theatre, the next order of business in rehearsal is often the identification of objectives (what a character wants) and actions (what she does to get what she wants). This is a non-useless relic of the abiding mid-century faith that the warp and weft of conflicting vectors of desire can constitute the fabric of a play. Some actors are more fundamentalist about this approach than others. They dislike and even avoid any kind of literary analysis of a play, believing that a single-minded pursuit of objectives is their best course. I do not take issue with this fundamentalism – maybe because I have precious ideas of my own – but I do not share it. I find that approaching a play as if every character is the hero of his own story can lead to intense but not necessarily deeply textured performance. I am what people call a 'character actor', and as such I enjoy thinking about performance from a slightly greater height. I use the rehearsal process in part as a chance to identify and expand upon characters' flaws – weakness, blind spots, folly – all to season that most delicious of dramatic treats, irony.

The best part of rehearsal – the crucial part, to my mind – comes in reckoning with others and reconciling my intellectually ideal performance with the reality of bodies onstage. I'm not sure that it isn't somehow good for the soul to spend a few hours a day observing and accepting and responding to the actions of others with genuine openness. One wishes to avoid excessive fruitiness in one's descriptions, but from the audience's perspective a play is a story, maybe, or a window on truth. From onstage, a play is an event in a room whose occupants all participate in the construction of meaning, in the distillation of signal from noise. In this, working on a Shakespeare isn't different from working on any other play. The process continues; there is no final product.

Training and influences

Alas, my training consists almost entirely of working on Shakespeare plays. Having some ability in music certainly never hurts with Shakespeare, and any movement background, be it dance, athletics, or something else, is useful in performance. I am an English major, both in undergraduate degree and in temperament, and I suppose I bring that way of thinking to my work.

My father never fails to observe how much my work owes to Warner Bros. cartoons, and there's truth in that, I guess. I find it hard to resist looking for the gag in just about any scene, and in my defense, Shakespeare's much-celebrated interpretability lends itself to comic readings. You might talk me out of putting an 'ew, gross' spin on Leontes' 'O, she's warm!' (*The Winter's Tale*, 5.3.109) but I wouldn't want to live in a world where Macbeth's ''Twas a rough night' (*Macbeth*, 2.3.60) isn't funny. I'm occasionally subject to the criticism that I am 'sending up' Shakespeare, though that is definitely not what I wish to do. I just believe that Shakespeare gives us the material to score a clean comic hit right in the middle of tragedy, and that the superimposition of humour atop pathos makes both richer.

If pressed, I might have to confess myself to be a Viewpoints actor, having worked with students of Anne Bogart (never with the great one herself), and having discovered that her systems of internal and external analysis mapped neatly onto my own far less hammered-out ideas about performance. I've always maintained a suspicion of any rhetoric of acting that includes words like honesty or truthfulness or authenticity, not because I think those concepts have no place in performance, but because I believe them to be related to the private, internal work of an actor whose outward work is necessarily a lie. I nevertheless encourage actors to polish up their 'reality of the moment' vocabulary because it's great stuff for chatting people up in bars.

Final thoughts

I know nothing about Shakespeare. I think it's important to reassert that every now and then, because humility in the face of such an artistic totality is indispensable. What I believe about Shakespeare is always subject to revision. His plays continue to confound us all, which is why we continue to produce and to write about him.

ALEX HASSELL, ACTOR

Verse

I feel very passionately about verse, and so I go over the verse first, breaking at the end of lines, and not breaking in the middle of lines, and mark the bits that seem irregular, or at least slightly different from a regular iambic pattern … like a sort of score … and of course there could be a number of options in the line and I would play with those options. It's a key, basically.

Before I'd done a lot of verse I used to practice different sorts of exercises that help get the verse into you: to physically beat it out, or walk it out, or pretending that you're throwing a dart into the wall on the final stress, so that you drive towards the end of the line and the end of the line becomes the most important thing and you find out why the end of the line holds the weight. It's an actor's job to try and become clever enough (by looking at the verse) to speak Shakespeare's lines rather than to make Shakespeare's lines fit into our miniscule understanding of the world, and I think the verse structure is one's guide to do that. If you look at a verse line and you think the verse is wrong because a stress falls in a place that you wouldn't usually stress it, it could be because you don't understand the line yet, the specificity of why it is that way, and what it means therefore to stress *this* word rather than *that* word.

It's a verse *pattern* rather than a verse *rhythm*, because a rhythm seems to suggest a tempo and a regularity of beat whereas a pattern is ... it's essentially the stresses saying, 'These are the most important words.' I definitely am not aiming for a soporific rhythm; I don't think the audience should know that they're hearing verse, they should just think they're hearing very clear erudite thoughts. In prose, I think that there should be a barely perceptible difference; you're certainly not aiming to go 'look everyone, we've changed from ...' but it will just sort of feel different, or seem different, if you know what I mean.

It takes an enormous amount of work to get really good at speaking verse. The basics can be learned in ten minutes, but to actually make it get past the phase when it sounds crap (as though you're hitting the emphases with a hammer) to when it no longer sounds like 'acting' and doesn't sound as though you are singing the verse ... that takes a long time. And I think most people give up before they get past that point, and they can't see that there *is* a place past that point, so most people think, 'Oh, I don't want to do that "versey" stuff because it just sounds all "versey" and rubbish.' But I think that only once you keep working past that point can you really reveal and live up to the full profundity and weight and worth and value of Shakespeare. To avoid working on the verse is as if you took the time signatures out of a piece of Beethoven or something like that. I can't understand ... it's baffling to me that people think that his words are the most important thing, the best in the whole world, but his verse: 'I don't really believe that.' Verse is the other half of his genius; it's giving you everything else.

To train yourself to be dextrous enough to think on the line – quickly enough, but not too quickly – and to hear and feel the words as you're saying them, and to allow them to impact upon you while trying to make them impact upon someone else, to be open enough to let them affect you, while not affecting them ... this takes a great deal of dedication and practice, and many actors don't want to do that. I think it's so important to make people passionate about verse for them to be able to bother doing all of the work that it takes, and drama schools don't always do that.

Verse speaking is so frequently coupled with voice work, and as much as I found a great deal of value in a lot of the voice work I did do at Central I felt its coupling with verse was just stupid, like 'if there's alliteration please God make sure you play the alliteration, and if there's a long vowel make sure it's really long so we really hear the emotion'. If the verse is written alliteratively and you say it out loud it *will be* alliterative, and that job is done by Shakespeare; you don't need to overegg the pudding. One of the biggest traps that you fall into is 'Oh, listen to how fantastically beautiful this bit is … I'd better try to do this bit lyrically'. What does that mean? That's when it sounds rubbish.

Emotion

It's important to avoid putting stuff on top of the performance, to avoid showing the audience how you're feeling. Emotion is essentially a by-product of getting or not getting what you want, and though sometimes you might slightly fake an emotion to try to influence someone, I think planned displays of emotion are beside the point in theatre. They are merely trying to con an audience into something or guide them into your understanding of the play or part, which I don't understand: why we would want to tell other people our understanding of the part? We should want them to come up with their own understanding of the part. What some directors want you to do from the very first scene is to come on and say, 'My character is a bit like this, now watch me be a bit like that for the whole play and not be surprised by me because I told you what I was going to do and what I'm like in the first scene.' I think they just pile crap on top of the play and on top of the parts so you don't see the play. You can't see the play, you can just see an actor masturbating and a director saying, 'I'm really clever, please give me another job.' If the audience are just given this sort of thing all the time the most they could feel is clever: 'Oh, I knew he was going to do that and he did do that', rather than being profoundly moved by the power of theatre. You have to be brave enough to not give the audience stuff all the time, and that is scary because that requires one to believe in one's own sort of natural charisma.

Action

I've done a bit of [the work of Sanford] Meisner, which is about putting everything on your scene partner, and that's similar to what I'm talking about with actions and verse. The actions – what you are trying to do to the other person – can be quite clear in Shakespeare, especially in verse. If you're looking at the verse you get a clearer and more specific understanding of those words, and it narrows down the options so massively. I suppose some actors might find that restrictive, but I don't at all; I think that's fantastic that it's so incredibly specific, that I must be playing only *this* sort of action towards my scene partner. Of course the way I do that would change in an infinite number of ways depending on what he or she had just done to me, and what was happening on stage in the moment.

I don't actually write down actions or anything like that – I have done that in the past – but actually I think that can become an academic exercise. Usually when I'm looking at a script what I'm trying to see with a line is: Why am I saying that line? What am I trying to change about the other person by saying that line? What is wrong with them or with this situation that needs to be changed by me saying the line? And then, depending on what's happening between me and the other person when that line comes up in rehearsing the scene, I figure out in the moment how to do it, as you do in real life. And I'll see how that happens, and why that happens, through knowing that each line has to be trying to change the other person and trying to end the play and the scene.

Character

Of course as many people have said, when you're working on a thrust stage – like the Globe or the RSC – the audience can and will do a lot of work for you if you 'cast' them. I also think who or what the audience represents for you can shift in a millisecond, but you begin from the same place you would with your scene partner on stage: 'What am I asking of them? How can they help me?' or 'What have they just thought about me which is wrong, that I now need to correct?' And the audience should be invited to change the course of how things unfold. In that sense, I think that 'character' is less orchestrated by the actor, and more in the perception of the audience. In real life no one walks about 'being their own character'. I try to think about doing less, and allowing your character to grow and be revealed as you go.

Tim [Carroll] often says, 'Don't play the information until you say it', meaning that you and the audience should all be together piecing this tapestry of information which is the play, together as we go. And if you start to play the information before it comes along in the text, then again there's no suspense, there's no need to say it. We talk about 'behaviour' a lot at The Factory, as in trying not to 'do behaviour' because that again is saying, 'Look what I'm going through, look at the sort of person I am, look what sort of world this is.' Coming into a scene with a focus on the previous circumstances and exhibiting behaviour connected with those is to feed the audience information that will then later diminish a line. For example, if it's supposed to be a hot day, don't come on 'playing hot' because then when you say 'it's hot' the audience will just go 'Oh right, that's what he was doing' rather than being surprised in any way.

In fact, it would be better not think about 'character' at all, when you're looking at the text, so then you can see more clearly that the text is riddled with inconsistencies and contradictions, just as any interesting human being is. If you begin by thinking 'Oh, what's my character like?' you then iron out all of these amazing inconsistencies: having the strength to *not* decide what sort of character you are and thereby limit it, and to search for as many inconsistencies and contradictions as you can is an immensely important thing.

But that's so hard to do, especially with Shakespeare. I once said to a brilliant well-known actor, 'Oh, I'm playing Cassio' and he said, 'Oh, the bookish one?' meaning, I suppose, the accepted way of playing it, or perhaps the way he played it … So much about doing Shakespeare is scraping away the crust and crud that has kind of been layered on top of it over the years. An idea of a character: 'I've always seen Hamlet like this' or 'I don't want my Hamlet to be like that, I want my Hamlet to be like this' or 'I don't want my Romeo to be really soft so I'm going to make him really hard'. That's got nothing to do with the text. And so many of the famous scenes that we see we think are 'The love scene' or 'The scene in which this happens' rarely actually *are* that because they're riddled with inconsistencies.

Shakespeare's verse is so brilliantly put together, it's really difficult to be dextrous enough to make it sound like real speech, and to have to try and mean what you're saying, and change the other person; those things are enough to think about, so there's no room in your mind for anything else. The verse line simply replaces any other thoughts that you have, and then there's no room for 'character'. In a sense, I think 'character' is what the audience perceives when they watch an actor do a bunch of stuff one after the other. And of course your character has parameters because they have the words on the page and that's it, and if you don't put loads of rubbish around the words on the page – rubbish that is your own invention of character – then the character will be revealed, and will change. If you don't hem it in, it won't be hemmed in. The only difference between you as a normal human being and you as an actor is that as an actor your thoughts are being replaced by ones that have been pre-written by a genius.

AMER HLEHEL, ACTOR

First steps with a script

My first step with a script, especially a Shakespeare text, is to understand the meaning, not the language, and to understand the characters. Shakespeare knew about *us*, he knew about humanity. He is a genius because of *that* – not just because he's a great poet. His characters are rich in human experiences and conflicts, full of oppositions; he's commenting on everything about you, and society, just in that character. Even the smallest characters in his plays are not one-dimensional or stereotyped in any way. So, my first step is to understand how Shakespeare sees my character.

When you say 'Caliban' to anybody who knows Shakespeare and knows *The Tempest*, the response is that Caliban is a 'monster' (*The Tempest*, 2.2.30), he is a 'mooncalf' (*The Tempest*, 2.2.109) and he is the villain in the play. However, when I started work playing Caliban at the RSC, I wanted to look for something else – the 'other' Caliban, my Caliban. Poetry-wise, he's got the most beautiful lines in *The Tempest*, and he's so connected to the island. He's a very emotional man and he's very aware that he is not being treated well by Prospero. So, I was looking for the human Caliban of Shakespeare and, to be honest, I found him much more human than just the villain or the monster – he's more than that: *They* look at him as a monster – as he looks at Stephano as a god.

I treated Caliban as I treat any character, which is to sympathize with him, not to judge him, but to love the character you are going to present on stage. I think back to drama school, one of my first ever teachers said: 'Don't judge your character, but love it', and I didn't understand that at the time. I thought, when you read, you see the whole picture of the play and your character is part of it, sometimes you read that your character is doing terrible things and so you judge. We have been taught to judge things in life from day one, so how can I not have an opinion on character? Then with practice and with working I learned how to love the ugliest characters you can meet. I think that's one of the most important things to know in acting: How to treat your character as yourself. We should be the villains, be bad and good; we should know how to love, hate and be jealous. If you can understand all this in yourself, as an actor, then you can understand everything in every character. You need to be your character's lawyer, advocate.

I was very much trained in the legacy of Stanislavski, however I think there is a missed part of Stanislavski's theory that people misunderstood. I don't believe in *feeling* things; I don't believe in *living* the character. The character lives in the lines and in the play. An actor needs to make it alive on stage, which is a step forward, and to make it human. So we have Stanislavski speaking about what you're feeling, what you're living, your thoughts – all the *Methods*. But how to put it on stage is the missed part of understanding Stanislavski. In theatre I don't *feel*. I just see things and my response is activated. I *see* (not *feel*, not *live*) what the lines say, then I can make them alive and vivid, then I can react. It's that famous line 'Acting is reacting' which is so true.

Somebody said that you have to learn a method, then throw it out and just leave it. The method will help you solve things, but don't go on stage and do things 'by the book'. Just be free, and be open, because there are other characters, and they also have actions, things they want to do, and they see things from a different point of view. You need to be open and part of the big story. The big story is much more important than your individual story, but you need to remember it is still about humans, it's about reactions, it's about inner-life and inner-thoughts. It's about actions and reactions from *other* people. If you do it in that way, then it's alive and it's now – it's happening now – and people can connect with it now. People love these plays because they are happening now.

Finding character

When it comes to finding character in Shakespeare, the language is so important – but it's the first step of doing a play, not the only one. Some people say Shakespeare wrote *everything* for you – you don't need to do anything; just read it correctly and it's there. I think that's not really true. I think Shakespeare wrote everything about the character, but he left for you everything about building *your* character – you can make *your* character and find *your* story. For me, that's what is brilliant about Shakespeare – any question that you want to know about your character exists in the script, but after that, it's yours to do with as you wish. I think Shakespeare would accept it when I say I don't do *Shakespeare's* Caliban, I do *my* Caliban. If you do it on stage, you have to do it your way – not Shakespeare's way.

When working on Caliban my first question was to discover: 'Who is Caliban, for me?' As a Palestinian it was easy to find it. A victim but, on the other hand, a victim doing some mistakes during the process of claiming freedom. So, similar to real life, it's becomes more and more complicated. People don't know his complete and real story, just as when they see news about a man with a covered face bombing a bus in Tel Aviv, bombing innocent people, he's a devil, he is a terrorist, he is inhuman. It looks like that. But the background ... why did that man reach that point? Why a man would decide to take others' *lives* and *his*? Most of the world can't see the big picture, but to see the bigger picture is essential, and to understand *why* a character does what they do is imperative.

To answer the big question: Did Caliban try to rape Miranda or not? I think Caliban didn't try to rape Miranda. I think there was a sexual tension and, in the beginning, sparks of love between Caliban and Miranda: Miranda, as a teenager, has curiosity. It's a man and a woman. Prospero saw that, and he stopped it before anything could happen between Caliban and Miranda. That's not Caliban forcing himself on Miranda. So that's *my* story.

On action

Stanislavski explained that you need to see things – don't feel, see. If you see things, your body will feel, and your senses will respond naturally. You can't decide for the character 'Oh, I'm sad now', because sadness is a result, and not the fabric of our experience and reaction to things; you need the process on stage to get to the result.

I try to ask myself in every line: 'What is my action?' So, when I say: 'The isle is full of noises, / Sounds and sweet airs that give delight and hurt not' (*The Tempest*, 3.2.135–6), what am I saying in that line? What's my action? I'm saying two things in that line; I'm saying to Trinculo and Stephano: 'Don't worry', and also saying, 'I am in love with this place'. So if I do both the result will be like a hunger, like I 'miss' something. So, it's about that by the end. If there is no action, then the line means only that this place is pretty. There is no goal in it. It's not my mission to describe, that is Shakespeare's mission – and he has done it so beautifully, it's all there. My mission is to put across another meaning – to be part of a story. In theatre, it's all about being part of the story, part of the action, having a goal and a need. It's about the need of Caliban to get his life back. The island is his life. So, let Shakespeare serve you, and then serve Shakespeare by bringing something unique. Then start to react to the others, because you are all playing together. The play is your home, is your God. So, you play in it – not outside it. Sometimes people jump outside the play! They act alone, act their decisions without considering anyone else on stage. Some actors try to jump out of the play because they want *their* play. That's why I don't like to start to decide things for the character before it 'happened'. *Caliban* and other characters will tell me how to walk, how to run, how to react, how my body should stand and sit, and that's what happened.

COLIN HURLEY, ACTOR

My ideal preparation would be to have the lines learned, the previous circumstances sorted, loads of yoga done, got fit, thin … and everything is there ready to go, so I can be free to play in rehearsal. The reality is I turn up to the first day of rehearsal cursing my family and my responsibilities, my laziness, the neighbours, all the things that stop me from being like Daniel Day-Lewis! I want to learn my lines before we start rehearsing, and unlike some actors I've never found that encourages me to 'set' anything at all: in fact you just come to rehearsals freer, because then you're 'looking up'.

Actioning is useful. I like to find a couple of actions in a speech, write them in the margins as options, a starting place, especially as a way of solving something that isn't working. I have worked with people who are very rigorous with this activity, but personally I find that a bit inhibiting, especially if the action found round the desk is seen as the last word on the subject. That moment solved. I'm happy to discover more useful actions in the space. That said, when I do workshops at the Globe, I do talk about the difference between adjectives and verbs: if I'm playing a King, 'Be more regal' isn't a helpful instruction. 'Squash them' or 'Dazzle them' with your words … that *is* helpful. It gives me something to *play*.

With Stanislavski's approach in general, I tend not to want to get bogged down with it, maybe I'm just lazy … but it *is* useful to have considered, for example, the given circumstances of the scene in a broad sense: have I just got out of bed? Have I just had a big meal? If I get stuck, then being more specific about those given circumstances is sometimes helpful. Unless

I'm really feeling like it on the day, I don't make a religion of asking myself what my objective is every scene. Sure, it'll be discussed in rehearsal. By performance time, I'm not sure it's useful for that to be a conscious thing. Hopefully absorbed, but not forgotten. Sometimes, though, if a scene stops working, it may be that we've been distracted, and need to polish up the set-up. It's all stuff to move us beyond recitation, not stuff to get too attached to. Fluidity over rigour, free playing and lightness over 'getting it right'. I don't want to show the audience my homework. Tools, not rules. When they stop being useful things to consider, drop 'em, or they can become bars on a cage.

I love the Mike Alfreds 'lists': what I say about myself, what I say about other people, what they say about me … that's fine prep to do at home, but I find it even better if you can bring that stuff into rehearsal, and say those things to those people, to their faces in the space, maybe in a kind of 'hot seat' set-up. Mike Alfreds describes it really well in his book *Different Every Night* (2014). Something about saying these things to someone outside the track of a scene, you're holding these descriptions up to the light, examining them out of context, some of the things you say and hear can ripple or resonate usefully. Perhaps the cumulative effect of hearing just what everyone else in the play thinks about your character can throw things up that may not be so obvious when reading or playing the whole thing from beginning to end. It goes a long way towards the whole company carrying the world of the play together.

Working with Tim Carroll at The Factory really helped me sharpen up the responsive side of working in the space with actors. He's the most enabling director I have worked with, he is playful, and *frees* actors, and is brilliant at spotting when you might be so busy playing your action that you missed an invitation from your scene partner. I think of it as learning to be on 'Receive' as well as 'Transmit'. Shows grow, change, morph. Sometimes a director may come back to see the show and 'take out the actors' improvements', whereas if Tim is 'in', I don't feel embarrassed that we may have discovered something new since he left. Playing what is actually there rather than what you had planned is useful. At the Globe this is more obvious: if, for example, somebody collapses in the yard and it's a big deal, it might be more appropriate to stop the play and deal with that situation before carrying on: we're all in the same space, and in that instant, if the drama in the yard overwhelms the drama in the scene, is it useful to ignore it? If we do that, we're not in the same space any more, and no one believes you.

When Mark Rylance was running the Globe, I think the emphasis was on 'actor-solutions' to the space: active listening, balancing the space, not getting caught between the pillars, talking *with* the audience, acknowledging that we are in the same space, and the listeners are all around us, and we must meet them all. When Dominic [Dromgoole] took over, because he is a director, we saw more emphasis on 'design-solutions' to the space: lots of additions to the stage, walkways into the yard and so on. Perfectly understandable. Directors spend much more time working with designers than with actors. I think that some of the 'design-solutions' I saw were rooted in a twentieth-/twenty-first-century idea of the theatre as a 'black box' which the designer can then put the world of the play into, whereas the actor-solutions of the first ten years of the Globe used the space 'as is'.

The thrust stage is a square peg in a round hole, that is, the theatre in the round. There isn't a 'front'. The pillars create a false proscenium, and this can lead us to 'playing out front'.

Thinking in terms of balancing the space is a useful way of sharing: when two actors are on the Globe stage and only one of them is speaking, we used to play a game whereby the speaker would move and listener would 'balance the plate' as the speaker moved around the circular space, to open up the speech to the various parts of the audience. After playing this game for a while we discovered that when the *listener* leads the movement, and not the speaker, the speech starts to feel more natural, as a series of responses to the movements and thoughts of the listener, and so the scene itself becomes far more exciting to watch. I bring that kind of game into workshops with students a lot, and it keeps the scene alive and playful. Basically, we're giving the listener permission to be an equal partner in the scene, the conversation. 'I've got the words, but you've got the punctuation'. The listener is punctuating the speech.

Teaching

I wish I had started teaching twenty years earlier than I did. Teaching workshops in drama schools has kind of completed the circle for me. There have been days when I have been teaching in the day, performing in the evening, when I'd remember what I had asked of my students, and would have to raise my own game, and practice what I had been preaching. If you want to really learn about something, teach it.

When I teach students, I notice that very often they feel under pressure in rehearsals, to deliver a result. There doesn't seem to be enough time, somehow. An approach I got from Tim was just running the play, but with specific objective, for example, telling the actors, '[W]e're running the play, but you have to say everything twice.' This never seems to fail to improve everything and everyone, because when you say a line twice, it becomes apparent that it is because the first time your scene partner didn't respond how you expected; it also buys you more time to think, and to respond. I think the 'great actors' are often those who seem to have 'more time', in the same way that great football players seem to have more time when they have the ball. So this game buys you more time in rehearsal – I call it 'Meisner-Lite' – and it usually seems to help us.

Actors will generally get to where you need them to be, if you give them permission to do so, and then shut up! Some might need a bit of help getting out of their own way, on occasion, but if we overload them with too many 'things to remember', how can we expect them to get up and play simply?

Practice makes playful

Because it relies on an initial element of private memorization of lines, rather than beginning with group rehearsal and 'table work', the model of rehearsal used at The Factory is perhaps in some ways closer to Shakespeare's own than might initially be thought. It is also the nearest thing I have experienced to being a true 'ensemble'.

Tim has us show up knowing only the lines, it's true, but when we are together we then have a lot of *practice*. If, instead of daily 'rehearsal', we have daily 'practice', whereby you train in the skills of listening and responding to what your scene partners are doing to you, accepting the offers that they make you, then you do find that you need comparatively little else. Tim's work seems very much about getting out of the way of the play, to let the actors and the audience meet each other, meet the play and to encourage them to discover, rather than decide, how the story will go.

T. R. KNIGHT, ACTOR

My very first action when working on Shakespeare is to stretch out my arms ... and reach for my well-loved *Shakespeare Lexicon* by Alexander Schmidt (1874). They are my crutches, volume A–M under one arm and N–Z under the other, and I lean on them heavily. Without an understanding of the text, all my other tools become useless. After I feel I have a grasp of the story, I set about breaking it down line by line, then scene by scene. I have never been a huge fan of a lot of table work with the whole company, some is necessary, but so much can be done outside the rehearsal room. That's my homework.

I start by first understanding the stresses and how they influence the line, finding how the rhythm either flows (or doesn't) depending on the character's emotional state, and finally, looking at how these small details affect the action of the scene. This process is as instrumental and necessary for me for interpreting modern language as it is in Shakespeare: moving through to the end of the line, linking thoughts as they bounce from one idea to the next and finding the antitheses. I use it every day I work, regardless of the style or genre of the text.

The next step of getting up on your feet and working with your director and fellow actors is most necessary, because it's only then that the play starts to expand and deepen and come alive. The language comes alive when approached on a physical level, and for this I often use exercises based on the work of Rudolf Laban and Jerzy Grotowski.

Approaching the text physically allows the electricity to spark, and to create a world where life can be both monstrous and beautiful. But most importantly, it will be relatable. Failing and stumbling is a part of the process, and sometimes it can give birth to exciting discoveries. I believe you can only truly affect your audience if they fully believe you, and for this to happen you need to embrace the structure of the text, as well as the emotion contained within it. Your responsibility to this audience is to take them along with you; when a 400-year-old text can feel like it was written yesterday, full of passionate longing or murderous rage, this journey can be genuinely thrilling.

I didn't go to a drama school, but rather learned through on-the-job training. For a long time my lack of schooling was an impediment to my confidence, especially when performing classical language. But, in the words of one of my mentors Ken Washington, '[T]here is more than one way to skin a cat.' Thankfully, I gathered he was speaking metaphorically! As the years have gone by, I have learned to appreciate my specific path and be grateful for it. I don't feel as though I belong to any specific tradition, but I have been heavily influenced by many people I have worked with, along the way: Elizabeth Marvel's performance as Rosalind in *As You Like It* at the Guthrie Theater in 1994 first opened me up to Shakespeare and 'rearranged' me in a way I never knew possible. As an American actor, I feel lucky to have also been taught by British practitioners, in particular Cicely Berry, John Barton and Jaq Bessell, who helped demystify language in such a humble and honest way, helping me clear the nonsense and baggage out of my way in order to set me on a path that continues to thrill and challenge me today. I think the distinctive thing about Shakespeare's language, and one of the reasons it still fascinates us so much today, is how perfectly it strikes our most primal chords.

Shakespeare is for everyone, to be spoken by everyone, no matter your education or dialect. I strongly believe that gender should not dictate casting, and anything that smacks of stale 'tradition' should be upended.

The true genius of Shakespeare is that it meets you halfway, bringing itself to you as much as you bring yourself to it.

ANDREW LONG, ACTOR

Working with Sam Mendes

If you don't at least take advantage of looking at the verse form rigidly when you begin, you're not allowing yourself the full capability of what's there for you. The thing I've discovered about Shakespeare is that these plays are hardy and sturdy and they can take almost anything that somebody wants to do with them, so I kind of have to adjust every time. It was interesting working on *Richard III* at The Old Vic directed by Sam Mendes. Once we'd done the first read-through that most are not fond of, he then worked on text line by line through the whole play. He would count out the verse, saying, 'That word would be pronounced this way' for every single part. By the second week he had Arabian carpets out and comfy chairs in a circle; and then we just kind of physically explored the play for a whole week like that. If you wanted to get up and move about you could. It wasn't improvising as such, it was using the text; if you knew it you can stand up and do it and if you still needed your script you could have it. It was just to explore the play, the physical life and your own journey. If you were mentioned in the script you had to stand up and that person would then talk directly to you, matching faces with names. It just was a free and easy exploration. Because of the way the economy has turned, you don't have that extra time to slowly explore, but you somehow manage to do these big, big plays in increasingly less time.

Before rehearsals begin

The prep work I do before the first rehearsal features a lot of reading the play; I scan the entire play, I go through and find the basic stuff: everything I say about other characters, what they say about me and how I talk about the world I live in. I then copy the punctuation from the First Folio on to my script. I also usually go through at least four different editions of the play just looking at the notes, because they are all different, and then I get as much information on to the page as I can before even I start reading it. This information is essential. I like to really sit with any poetic device I can find; I try to find things like repetition of sound and rhetoric before I get to the first read through. There are many discoveries to be made; you can find out that there are thirteen 's's in a couplet, which I don't think that's ever an accident, and begin the conversation about what that means and how you will convey that meaning.

Physical approaches

My physical work when exploring character can be something as simple as investigating where a character holds his tension, where his gestures begin from or what shoes he has on – those are all huge things. If you're playing someone like Richard III you would have to really think long and hard about what he's actually suffering from, what's debilitating about it and how that is going to make you move. However, it's usually just something simple that opens up a door and ends up taking you down a particular road for a character. I find something I like and then I layer it in to the play in different places. Sometimes these decisions don't always come from the director or the costume department, so I think long and hard enough about it that I give myself a direction to work in.

In fact, the teacher that I gleaned the most from in graduate school was my movement teacher, Carol Thompson. She made me more self-aware about what's specifically unique to my body, down to the sizes of my bones and how that affects the physical choices I make. Once I became aware of the things that I do habitually, then I could choose whether to maintain or change those things, whereas before I don't think I ever thought that way. The knowledge she passed on was helpful.

My work is a combination of gut and technique; it's never one or the other, it's a symbiotic thing. Any given production is usually a melting pot of different styles and experience levels. The director's job to mould all those people and styles into one unified mode of storytelling.

Working with Michael Kahn

Michael Kahn is the perfect example of a great storyteller. He makes the play better every day you work on it. He's totally consumed by the play while he's working on it. He usually knows the whole play, knows every line of text in it and he sees everything that happens on that stage; person number 36 in the corner can scratch their nose and he'll go, 'Why did you do that?' and he's formidable like that. For his process he spends a good amount of time at the table and then he goes through staging the play. Once he's staged it, he wants you pretty much off book straight away. The people that can respond to that kind of pressure he won't worry about, and the people that do struggle will be where his focus will go until, eventually, everyone is going the same speed. Then, when he releases the play, he's done. On to the next project. Like a switch.

Shakespeare in different spaces

Looking back on the work I've done and the things I haven't really explored yet, I would love to do something very small, like in a black box. It'd be great to tackle one of these big plays but with a really small group of actors in a black box theatre. I've done a lot of these huge plays in the bigger houses with casts of thirty-five/thirty-six but to be able to experience the same stories when the audience are so close to you would be exhilarating. In that setting, you can allow yourself to use a completely different set of tools; that's the joy of doing a contemporary play when I get those opportunities. It's like the difference between working outside with just your voice, and working outside with the microphone where you're amplified; it allows you to do different things and utilizes a completely different instrument. To be able to do this epic poetry in a whisper is something you just couldn't do in a 1,200-seat theatre, but that opportunity is something I'd love to have.

Performing in bigger venues is more like an athletic endeavour, I don't think people realize the kind of support and physical effort it takes to get that muscular language out to 1,200 people unamplified. You still have to do those smaller moments that might seem intimate, but make them so supported that they can travel across the space.

I was privy to a conversation Kevin Spacey was having with his sound designer at the Old Vic. The sound designer was telling Kevin that he had noticed over time how he has mastered the unique demands of playing The Vic: specifically, he knew where you need to pitch your voice, on to what physical structures in the building to bounce your voice back from and so on. These things he just didn't know how to do when he was first starting his tenure. I remember Kevin trying to do the same thing when we were in Epidaurus, getting his voice into the aisles, using them as a sounding board for his voice. Epidaurus holds about 14,000, and that amount of bodies can easily soak up all of the sound. You really have to use gesture too, or people in the back simply won't know who is talking. So, when we came back from Epidaurus, the play was better. The Old Vic suddenly felt more manageable. As a company we had built a capacity to speak to 14,000 people, so taking it back to the 1,200 capacity of the Old Vic meant that the play could breathe more. That's the exciting thing about playing in so many different venues; you're always going to find a new wrinkle.

Teaching

These days I'm more interested in the verse structure and in punctuation than perhaps I once was. I think you're neglecting something if you don't sit in the structure of the way it's written first. You can hear the sense of the speech just by saying the first and last stress of each line. Looking back over my own training, I have tried to take something from every class, or every teacher I've ever had, even the ones I haven't particularly liked. I also learn though my own teaching work – I teach regularly, and this refreshes my connection with the techniques and the exercises I was trained with. Teaching also makes me realize that not everybody thinks in the same way. Some people can be wonderful technical actors, but perhaps they struggle with big emotions … and sometimes it's the other way around.

I like that place that teeters on rage or tears but does not quite fall prey to it, supported by your technique – I mean you still have to talk! These are big plays with big moments that challenge you and they require a bold actor that cares about what he or she is saying. That is the most common note I give while teaching: care more.

JONATHAN McGUINNESS, ACTOR

Auditions

When it comes down to process, you do some of the work before you've even been hired. Obviously, for the audition, you'll be focusing almost exclusively on the journey of the character you're auditioning for, so you'll pick up lots of first impressions of the character. You try and get a grip on what other characters say about that character, where they fit into the whole story and then, I suppose you'll probably really focus in on one little bit, a scene, or even a speech. Then you go over that in quite a lot of detail, and then you'll go in and audition. I also like to use the time before rehearsals begin as an opportunity to keep reminding myself of the scope and sense of the whole play, and what that story is. Then you come to the rehearsal and that's a whole different thing really. Once you begin to rehearse, you start to focus on your own character and your own scenes; this is what most of the work is about for you, when you're in a rehearsal room.

Rehearsals

I personally try to come in with ideas; it's strange, because though you want to have ideas, you *don't* want to be locked on to those, because, if all the elements in rehearsals are good, you can go off on a complete tangent and a journey with something that can be 180 degrees opposite to what you first thought it might be. It's nice to be able to just come in and start that whole journey together, particularly if it's somewhere like the RSC where you do sort of have time. I mean I've worked at places where you have three-and-a-half weeks to get a show together and the design is done, the director has almost said,

'Right, you know, you're going to enter from there, the light's going to be like that, we've got this amount of time, I need you to be off book by here, and we've got, this is how it's going to be' … you know where you stand in that framework!

I suppose the rehearsal process usually begins with a read through, so you start hearing the text aloud. You've been doing it all with your own voice in your head and then you hear other actors speaking those other lines, which is always interesting. At about this time, you will probably be given a sense of the different design elements, and then you start playing about with those ideas. Then, as the rehearsals continue, you experiment with things which may not explicitly get in the show, but which might implicitly find a way in, and bubble to the surface at any given point. And it's weird, because, you can almost have a sugar rush of ideas. The director might say, 'Try it like that', and you do it, and it works really well and you really enjoy it; then, two weeks later, the enjoyment of that idea has gone, and you're thinking, 'This just feels really crap now.'

This is always an interesting time for the show, because it is when things settle down and you start realizing, 'Actually, this doesn't feel truthful', and by 'truthful' I don't mean naturalistic. I just need to know why I'm doing everything I'm doing. If I have that, I can go out and do it with confidence. But, if I have to go on stage not really believing in it, I can get away with that for a little bit, but then as the role goes on I sort of lose confidence in it. And then you lose confidence in the whole thing, in some way. I suppose the luxury of having a long rehearsal period is you've got the time to try and look at everything there, and every bit of the play gets a little bit of love and attention.

Stanislavski, subtext and Shakespeare: what you feel, you say

When it comes down to methods and processes, I think almost all modern actors have been influenced by Stanislavski, even if they believe that they are in no way, shape or form a method actor or a Stanislavski follower. That's because it is what we all do now, it's ingrained through training and experience: we all ask, 'Why am I doing this?' and regardless of what you call them, you play objectives in some way. I think actors have probably always done this, but Stanislavski formulated a method around those practices, and he only did that to feed actors' imagination: he always said his system was to help you when you come up against problems and your imagination isn't firing on all cylinders: it wasn't supposed to be a rigid set of rules.

Of course when we try to tie Shakespeare and Stanislavski together, there is the issue of subtext. Stanislavski is so interested in the subtext, and what is not being said. So, using his method you are invited to mine all of that out from under the text, whereas in Shakespeare I'd say generally subtext doesn't exist. That suggests you don't need to approach Shakespeare from such an intellectual place.

What's fascinating with Shakespeare is this notion of 'what you feel, you say'. So the trick is waiting until the thought hits you, and then you can say what you feel. I suppose you can easily fall into the trap of trying to play things from later on in the play. In *Richard III*, for example, he doesn't become the villain until he says he's going to kill everyone to get the crown. Before that, he's not a villain, and when he has that thought, 'This is what I'm going to do', he hasn't been sitting in his room planning it: the thought happens when he says it, in that moment. So I suppose the subtext comes in the form of soliloquies: that's when these characters reveal their secret inner workings. It's all there for you, you don't have to worry about, 'Oh, what else am I?' because Shakespeare gives you all the information you need. What you say is what you're thinking and feeling. Shakespeare hands it all to you. His plays start at Level 10. Even a comedy such as *A Midsummer Night's Dream* starts with the predicament of Hermia either entering an arranged marriage or being executed. Shakespeare is so good at keeping those stakes high and dramatic, we have to find a way to bring some sort of emotional truth to that language.

Language and character

In truth, I don't really approach the language technically. I think the technical tools can really help, but it isn't my first place to go when starting a new process. When I started working with Ed Hall – who's very into the verse – I found it really hard initially to master all the verse speaking techniques that he talked about, but once I had, I found them useful, and something that I could call on when needed. In fact there is something about the technicality that can really help. If someone's doing verse well, I'm usually not aware of it being verse, because iambic pentameter is a very natural kind of rhythm, as in 'I'm going to go and get a cup a tea'. Verse may be something actors think they have a problem with, more so than audiences. In fact, the language can also give you a drive into the scene for free. The language gifts you the stakes. Once you get the rhythm it carries you along a bit, but that's not what I think about first. I find my starting point usually is about the emotions of what's going on between the characters.

Orsino in *Twelfth Night* spends so much of the play infatuated with Olivia, and then right at the end he changes, and loves Viola. Some people say that's a bit ridiculous, but to me that's completely understandable. He's almost like a kind of addict, he's obsessed with this woman who he basically doesn't know, he's like a teenage boy. He's in love with the idea of being in love. Then when reality hits home, when he actually meets Olivia, and she says the things she says to him, it completely punctures him. So he realizes that he was wrong. I actually think it's sort of completely truthful. Of course it's also ridiculous, but then that's love, that happens. People get completely obsessed with something and they can't see the wood for the trees. That's what I love in Shakespeare's plays: all the characters have extremes, and do extreme things.

Shakespeare was an actor, writing for other actors who he knew. You can really tell that when you work on it. For me, 99 per cent of rehearsal is about being in the moment with the other actor, discovering what is happening dramatically. For me, the ideal rehearsal is one in which the director creates an atmosphere where nobody is afraid to follow their instincts, where you can enjoy just doing lots of stupid things without being worried that they're right or wrong. Then it's the director's job to push you in certain directions: 'that's terrible', or 'try that', or 'keep that in'. It's out of those moments that unique moments emerge, and those are the things specific to the rehearsal room, they aren't something that you can predict from working alone.

When you've been doing a play for a long time, and the words actually are so deeply ingrained, you're no longer thinking about them. It's a bit like driving, in that when you learn to drive it seems really complicated, and you think, 'How will I ever get this?' But after a long while, you become really alert, and you do everything you're supposed to do, but you're also able to think about things and talk to your passenger. So, if you're doing a long run of a play, you've got a chance to get the work so deeply in your body that you're not ever thinking about your next line, and you can actually be really in the moment. With some actors you can find that little things change – small stuff that an audience who watched it two nights on the trot probably wouldn't even notice – but these changes can help things feel quite different and alive, which is what makes it fun to perform.

PIPPA NIXON, ACTOR

As far as the 'first layer' of work goes, I don't like making too many decisions before I go into the rehearsal room. I know some people that do: they really do make decisions on who they are before entering the rehearsal room, and then when they are in the rehearsal room they use that time to polish up those choices. That's not part of my process, but I do like to have gone into the first day of rehearsals having an idea of a history of who that character might be; the world which they come from. For example, when I was cast as Dorothea in *Cardenio* at the RSC, because I knew the play was partly based on *Don Quixote*, I read *Don Quixote*. There is a section in the novel where Don Quixote meets Cardenio – and the story involves Dorothea – and this gave me a great background and starting point. Greg [Doran] likes to do lots of research as part of rehearsals, so I photocopied all of the Don Quixote episodes that had Dorothea in them. With our text, I felt that there were gaps about that character, so I stuck in all of the missing pieces about Dorothea to join up the journey, so that I knew what she was doing when she wasn't present in the play and when I was offstage. I wanted to bring something of myself to her, but also keep her as consistent with the source as possible.

I think I like to look for that sort of continuity in most cases. When I did *A Midsummer Night's Dream* – although that production was set in the 1960s – I still made sure that I knew who Hippolyta/Titania was in her classical Greek context. Then I began to look for ways I could relate that to the 1960s woman in our production: Nancy Meckler (the director) had set the play in a very underground, Mafioso world, with both Hippolyta/Titania and Theseus/Oberon as 'drug-lords'. They were both warriors, both ran big 'armies' and both would kill. And so, to start creating the character, I went back to the original source, to find the essence of who she was, before then building upon someone's conceptual 'take' on the piece. I would do that with anything.

Actions

At some point in the rehearsal period, you have to be mechanical and go: 'Right – I have to make some very strong choices here', and then, as you begin to actually play with these choices in rehearsal, it becomes less of a question of just playing actions, you find that once you manage to iron out all the technicalities you've put in place, you can find a character that can live and breathe. First you have to invest in those choices, but then when someone plays something towards me, I want to be able to respond to that, rather than fit their actions into the mechanics of what I've already built. Things have to be able to change. It's no good getting stuck in a choice that you have made. For example, the reason I enjoy playing with someone like Alex Hassell is because we're both responsive and brave in the choices that we make on stage. So it is very playful and lots of discoveries are made through 'play'.

I've also got an action book (Caldarone and Lloyd-Williams, 2004) – and sometimes when I do feel really stuck and think, 'Oh, there's got to be a more interesting way to play this', I'll look through and go, 'That action, OK, I'm going to try this' – but, at the same time, it's fine to let that go if it doesn't work for you. For example, during the first week of rehearsals for the 'Ill met by moonlight proud Titania' scene (A *Midsummer Night's Dream*, 2.1.60–145), Nancy [Meckler] wanted us to action it, but I did not feel ready to do that, because I felt like I was still at the stage where I'm was feeling out exactly what each line meant. She wanted me and Jo [Stone-Fewings] to pin down what we were doing to each other. I thought to myself: 'I've no idea. I haven't been able to get on stage and play with Jo enough to know what I want to do to him with this speech.' But I went along with that idea, and we actioned it, and then we went up and played it, and of course the actions we had penciled in completely changed – because Jo would do something to me that would make me react in a completely different way. But then, amazingly, what did happen, is by the end of that eight weeks, I came back to some of the actions Nancy wanted me to make in the first place. But I needed to explore the scene fully for myself, first.

I remember Greg [Doran] saying in rehearsals that there are certain words that come up, often, in this script, and one of them was *honour* ... and for Dorothea, that word is like her soul: it's all about *honour*. I say the word 'honour' about three or four times in one particular scene with Alex, and I just think ... whatever happens between me and Alex in that scene ... I have to keep coming back to that word. Actually, once you've done all the hard work, you sort of want to throw it away and to be able to play – and to take a word with you into that game is quite helpful. So, whatever my actions are, they have to be *honourable* to myself and towards him: and that enables you to play anything, as long as you come back to that. It's not about playing a generic word: *Honour … Love*, whatever – it's about connecting to words that are deeply rooted in the soul of the character. That you have discovered through out the rehearsal period and the playing of it on stage.

Verse

I worked at the Globe for three seasons, and did verse and text work there with Giles Block – who is wonderful, so brilliant. I think there *are* rules: the thought has to go to the end of the line, for example, rather than trail away at the end, as can happen in contemporary speech. I think it is important to know the beat – the iambic pentameter – and that is different from speaking in our natural, modern speech patterns. So, I go through the script and mark all the stressed lines – I completely scan it – and I mark it with a dash and a little slash to find out the key words to stress, and mark out the length of the thought, which is often indicated by punctuation.

But I know there are some actors who are fundamental about verse line endings, and, as I said before about character work, it has to be about the truth more than the technique, so … I think you need to have the technicalities in place, but if I don't fall on every stressed word, I don't beat myself up about it. I try and bring out the last word of each line, because that's often really important, and because you have to respect and honour the poetry of the verse. But once you know the mechanics of it … then you can start playing. I think I'm learning to do that, and I hope that I am getting better, technically, at working with the verse, but I don't want to be strictly obedient to the technicality of the verse, at the expense of investing in the character.

There is a Katie Mitchell exercise which involves scanning the whole play, all of your lines and other people's lines to ask the following: What does my character say about themselves? What do I say about other characters? What do other characters say about me? It makes you look at the text from your character's specific viewpoint in a very detailed way and pick up clues about who they are.

Your character is in the text, but also, as I said before, you have to bring all of yourself and invest in that text because when the text becomes inhabited, it comes alive. You have invested it within yourself and within all the other research that you have done. In some ways the research that I might do gives the text a context or a visual journey in which to run. For example, Titania's speech 'the forgeries of jealousy' (*A Midsummer Night's Dream*, 2.1.81–117) is so full of imagery, and so I went out and found the images – there is a 'nine men's morris' down by the river in Stratford, for example – and for those I couldn't find I scoured the internet for images – and I put these images up on the walls of my room, alongside the lines of that particular speech associated with those images. These stayed up well into the run of the production. I still have all those images somewhere in my mind.

Another thing I wanted to say is that actors are instinctive, and we need to trust our instincts, and often when you first read a text, and get a first idea of a character, you are often right, and you do come back to it. But there are other things that can enrich it, and make that initial impulse or idea about the character grow and grow. I think an actor needs freedom. I think an actor freaks out when they are not given that freedom: it's a very exposing job. The rehearsal room needs to be protected: it should be a place where you can fail, and you can make mistakes. I notice my own habit: within a four-week rehearsal process, always in week three – I get to this crisis point where I don't know what the hell I'm doing! It is traditional! I think every actor goes through that, like: 'I am the worst actor in the world', and when it happens I tell myself: 'Ah! You've hit that point! Just keep going, keep going!' and somehow, by the time you're at the tech., it's going to start coming together. Previews are a great place to formulate decisions and to see if the audience is following your story so that by opening night you think, 'OK I am ready for this to be presented.'

It comes down to breathing . . .

Speaking the text – the way that Shakespeare wrote it – absolutely corresponds to the way in which we breathe, and I think the more an actor can be comfortable with breathing onstage, the better they're going to speak that verse. When you breathe properly your voice drops into its natural resonance, and it is not constricted, and you are connected to your diaphragmatic breathing and that enables you to articulate the language, which is so muscular. I wonder whether, if you abandon yourself to the text, and have the technique behind you and start to inhabit the text ... that it might start changing you ... working on you, transforming you.

You do all this work in the rehearsal room, so that in performance the words can have a life of their own. If you are with an actor onstage, and are both listening and responding to each other, something can happen that you can never ever get back again, a magic happens, where you are completely in 'flow' and in the moment. You hit on 'genius'. You feel it and the audience feels it and you are all 'one'. That's what we are in the business for.

JULIET RYLANCE, ACTOR

First steps

This may be the most obvious answer in the world but ... the very first thing I do when working on a Shakespeare play is to find a quiet place, consciously clear my mind of any preconceptions I have about the play, and then read it. Twice. I give myself permission to embark on a journey of discovery, with only the script as my map.

My first read is to experience the play as an audience member might, seeing and hearing it for the first time. I note where I am moved, or when I suddenly find myself laughing out loud; when I'm inspired or brought to tears. I make notes of my experience and then take a few hours, a day maybe, to see how the play stays with me, in what way it has changed me, how its themes feel relevant to my life today and the world around me.

The purpose of my second read is to focus solely on my character's journey through the play, noting both the physical and emotional arc of my character's particular journey through the story. Like life, we begin our story in one place, both physically and emotionally, and end in another. I mark these key moments of change and discovery.

This simple exercise is to discover my instinctual and emotional response to the story and my character's journey through it. For me this is key to unlocking a Shakespeare play, and whatever work I do from this point on needs to be in service to the themes and teachings of the story as I perceive it as a whole. These great Shakespearean works resonate differently, I feel, according to the social and political climate in which they are performed. So, this first read is an exercise in freeing me to explore it at this specific moment in time.

These initial notes become a foundation, a starting point, one I will refer to again and again throughout the course of a rehearsal process and in performance, particularly so during a long run of a production.

Language

Shakespeare's masterly use of blank verse and prose, antithesis and metaphor define the language of his writing, and are the greatest opportunities and challenges that Shakespeare gives us as actors. When Shakespeare chooses to use verse instead of prose, or 'thee and thy' instead of 'you and your' these are clues, tools for understanding intent, or importance of a moment, or simply education or class. The puzzle is challenging, but the discovery of a potential reason for each choice is electrifying and a direct aid to 'playing'.

Verse can feel daunting, particularly as there are so many opinions about how it should be spoken. But I remind myself that it is also the most natural thing in the world. Iambic pentameter: the iamb; this is the simple rhythm of a heartbeat. Five heartbeats to a line. I make a point of listening to people speak around the city and so often, without knowing it, the pattern of their speech naturally emerges as a perfect iambic pentameter. It's somehow part of our oral history, our blood, our breath. This fascinates me, and encourages me. Yes, a good drama school education is invaluable as it gives one three years of exploration and practice, of getting one's head and mouth around speaking verse, of building up the dexterity to keep it up for three hours at a time … but nature and confidence also play their part.

What I love most about verse is the structure it gives one within which to play. I think of Shakespeare works like great symphonies, each script made up of a series of notes, pitches and rhythms. And just as a pianist would learn a score by painstaking practice, playing the same refrain over and over again many times a day to get each tiny section right, we actors need the same kind of discipline. Repetition with diligence and precision is necessary, until it becomes familiar and natural. Moreover, the more skilled we become with verse as our foundation, the more able we are to make discoveries and new choices. We begin to see extreme variations in sentence structure and length, we make decisions about how to handle a run on line, how to play a caesura caused by punctuation midway through a line, how long a pause we might allow at end of the line or how fast the inhalation of breath … Like a great jazz pianist might play with syncopation, the off-beat, playing with these forms can be used to galvanizing effect. The opportunities are limitless. What makes Marta Argerich's performances of Chopin so extraordinary? I think this kind of alchemy is created from the fusion of complete dedication and devotion to form, with a complete abandonment in the moment, whatever it may bring.

Discovery, preparation and play

My practice could be condensed into three stages: discovery, preparation and play. Discovery is those first couple of days I've described, of reading, responding and marking the large brushstrokes of the story in my imagination. Preparation is next; a series of written and spoken exercises that help get me ready for the rehearsal room. I like to give myself at least two weeks for this. I begin by making three lists: what my character says about herself; what she says about others; what others say about her. This gives me a very clear idea of who she is, how she feels about herself and how she interacts with the world around her. From this list I begin to work out her super objective through the story. What drives and moves her forward through the play, how that is changed or enforced by certain events that happen in the play and how she deals with them. The final step of this written homework is actioning. For me my aim is to action each line as a guide to performance, but I usually wait to do this until we are in week two or three of rehearsal, so as not to lock down or block myself from allowing new impulses to emerge with my fellow players, led by our director. I normally will make a few lists of three similar actions per line and play with them and see what feels right when. For me, actioning needs to be very fluid: how a fellow actor gives you their line will and should determine the action you use in response.

Next for me in this preparation phase is to begin lifting the words of the page … I just begin saying the verse out loud, sometimes in pace with my pulse. Even if it doesn't always scan, I keep to the pulse – surprises emerge for me this way – sometimes a stress that one might imagine won't work, surprisingly does, which is thrilling. I think sometimes the most interesting choice is to try not to break the verse, but perhaps to keep trying it in the iambic rhythm to see if a discovery can be made. For example, many of Shakespeare's soliloquies begin with 'O': 'O, what a noble mind is here o'erthrown!' (*Hamlet*, 3.1.149). Most would surmise that the O is a trochee and should be stressed. But because we have no definite evidence for what should be a trochee or not, I like to see if it might be more interesting to let it alone … saying it out loud, choosing not to invert the stress … I love how it changes the playing of the line. The O becomes a springboard, a jumping-off place to get to the meaning of the line. It feels beautifully simple and active. That's exciting to me. Next, I do the opposite, saying the line breaking the natural rhythm and inverting the stress, (stressing the O) and I realize that suddenly the line feels more emotional, slower, that the most important thing might be how I feel about his mind being overthrown rather than his mind being overthrown. It perhaps also sounds a little indulgent? I feel both choices are valid, neither is wrong. A director may prefer the trochee in this case. In another case the director may not. But this part of preparation for me is about generating possibilities. Even if I decide to use the trochee and stress the O, I might be more conscious of not indulgently wallowing in the O but keeping a forward momentum through the line.

Playing with the words at home like this – in the shower, whispered in bed at night, out of breath while running – is a wonderful way to explore and ready oneself for rehearsal. I won't learn them at this stage but they become my own this way without being bedded down, solidified into an acting choice.

Being 'in play'

The final stage and the most rewarding is stepping into the rehearsal room. I used to be quite scared of the rehearsal room.

Having been fortunate enough to watch many rehearsals as a child of parents in the theatre, it took me a while to really emerge and accept my place as an adult in the room. I give myself license now to *play*. And in play, nothing can really be wrong, just more or less interesting a choice. Play means whatever the director wants to do, wants to explore, what games the cast want to play as a way into a scene. This will usually consist of scene work, breaking down the beats of each scene, establishing the changes in direction, discovering what the conflict or obstacle in the scene may be, and how each character in it might try to overcome that obstacle. Often, we will use games to explore that scene work, such as improvising around the situation: perhaps the 'scene' that came before that isn't in the play, it's something unwritten, and has to be imagined. Or perhaps someone feeds you your lines (before you know the script); this is a wonderful exercise as you experience being truly present, not knowing what you're going to say next. This period of play may include the exercise known as 'hot seating': the group of players ask one actor questions about their character's life and s/he needs to answer them, in character. Play may consist of throwing a ball at the end of your line to the person you're speaking to, or having to move to a new position in the room before saying a line to another actor. This is really where a play begins to come to life. It is thrilling and surprising, sometimes terrifying, but it is where alchemy hopefully begins to happen, being 'in play'

Training and influences

A good warm-up is essential. Just like an athlete preparing their body for a race, so too we prepare ours for the stage. Voice work is perhaps the most important part of my training for Shakespeare, so I can use the breath, and access the different parts of the voice in the body to convey different things. I loved studying Stanislavski at RADA and I think his teaching has become integral to my process as an actor. The need to speak, the need to change something … and of course, the importance of actions, as I mentioned earlier.

I wish I knew or could say to what tradition my work belongs; to be honest … I don't know. I know that I've been inspired and influenced by my parents' work, and their ongoing, evolving exploration of Shakespeare's works. I was fortunate enough to grow up in and around rehearsal rooms, watching and absorbing what was going on, as a child. Later, the Globe Theatre has been a major influence to me in the playing of Shakespeare, the shared light creating a shared experience; the relationship with the audience being alive and active, with actors treating the audience like another player on the stage. Jaq Bessell, Tamara Harvey, Tim Carroll and Arin Arbus have all influenced my playing of Shakespeare immensely, and Matthew Warchus, Simon McBurney and Complicité, and Robert Lepage and Peter Brook have been hugely influential in forming my aesthetic and contemporary relationship to the making of a play, and a production.

JONATHAN SLINGER, ACTOR

Text

The first thing is to make sure you understand every single syllable of it, in a very rigorous, very ruthless way. I think one reason that some people may not understand Shakespeare when they come and see it is because the actor doesn't really understand what they're saying. I think you have to be absolutely ruthless, going through it syllable by syllable, with a fine-tooth comb: there are so many layers, so many textures, so many levels, so many hidden meanings, so many words that are familiar to us, but that have changed their meaning completely over time. It's important to have understood those different ways of interpreting the line, before making a decision. I'd say, even when you *think* you know what they mean, check again!

Greg [Doran] will devote the first two weeks of rehearsals to text work with the whole company, making sure everybody understands every single word in the play. Michael [Boyd] works slightly differently: he takes it scene by scene, working only with the people who are in that scene; at the end of that session Michael gets it up on its feet. He feels that the sooner in the process you get the work up on its feet, the better. Certainly, all of the best Shakespearean directors I've ever worked with will do an intensive period of working out what the text means, and I think that's hugely important.

Actions

I'm not rigorously technical about actioning. Some actors will take apart their script for meaning, then they'll take apart their script for beats or units, then they'll take apart their script for actions: they might assign an action for every line, every single moment, and this might result in pages and pages of transitive verbs. I don't tend to do that. Actioning is something that I will start to do only if I don't know what I'm doing in a scene. In my view, the actioning is inherent within the writing somehow; people's objectives, people's super-objectives – it's all clear in a piece of good writing, and that's why Shakespeare's so great to play.

Establishing character

Once I've worked out what the character is saying, my process is then a dual one, attending to the external and the internal aspects of the character. I will start to make some decisions before rehearsals begin: these tend to be just thoughts and ideas that I've had. Once rehearsals begin, many decisions are made in a more organic way, they just sort of happen as you rehearse. Partly it's a physical thing, in that you have to discover the external aspects – how the character moves, how they stand, and also how they sound – but all of those things can be informed by the most important thing, which is the internal stuff: the psychological mapping, working out psychologically who these characters are, why they are, what drives them, what their motivations are and what has created this character before the play begins. I've found it important and helpful to work out the character's past, background history, relationships with family members and so on.

Richard III's relationship with his mother was a very interesting one that I wanted to unlock to some degree. She's noticeable by her absence, particularly in *Henry VI Part 3*, where we hear about Richard III's birth, which apparently was this hugely ominous, portentous, horrible event: with people screaming and women fainting at the birth of this creature. So, you get an idea that all is not right between mother and son, and that was really interesting to me. I wondered what it would do to a person if their mother rejects them and says, 'I can't believe I've created this horrible monster.'

With Macbeth, similarly, I was trying to find the nub of his ambition. Maybe some people are just born with an ambitious gene, but I wanted to nail it down to something a bit more specific.

In a biography about the real Macbeth, we found that his grandfather had been a powerful, successful king who had also seized the crown by killing the previous king, and who had then ruled for thirty years. His father, on the other hand, didn't become king, was militarily unsuccessful and was constantly having to ask Macbeth's grandfather for help. I suddenly got this image of Macbeth's father, in Macbeth's eyes, being a weak man who didn't continue the grandfather's legacy, and it occurred to me that maybe Macbeth wants to reclaim the throne, and bury the memory of this weak, vacillating father. That was very useful, because suddenly I could put into context why Macbeth wants the throne as much he does.

Internal dialogue

Once you've opened the production, then it becomes about mapping out the character's internal dialogue. Every human being, I believe, has an internal dialogue: sometimes you speak your thoughts and your thoughts align with what you're saying; at other times, it is the antithesis of that, and you say one thing while thinking something very different. Either way, there is a thought process fizzing away, and so I like to map out exactly what my character is thinking throughout the course of that play. So, you could stop me at any point during a production's run and say, 'What are you thinking now?' and I would be able to tell you exactly what my character's thinking.

Shakespeare's characters will very often be duplicitous and have scenes where they're saying things that they don't mean, but typically they will have a moment during which they reveal to the audience exactly what they're really thinking. Richard III is a particularly acute example of this kind of character, of course, but we constantly have to contend with what's going on in our head, and we have to say. There's great theatrical value in watching somebody struggle between the two, having difficulty stressing what's really going on in their head, or watching somebody desperately try to not say the thing that they want to say.

Of course, this is, and should be, a very fluid thing. A character's internal dialogue is not the same at the end of a run of a play as at the beginning as it becomes more refined and nuanced with every performance. It is important for an actor to stay in the moment to allow for such development. One way of doing this is to continually remember to *listen* to the other actors on stage. If your focus is completely on the other characters, you will never not be in the moment.

Using the audience

Working at the Globe revealed the importance of interaction with the audience to me. It's the only theatre we have in this country which fosters that kind of immediate response. It made me realize for the first time that writers of this period were writing with that dynamic in mind; questions are directly asked of the audience, and so the audience might well have responded directly. That then begs the question: if the audience are essentially another character in the play, then what are they? Who are they? What are they thinking? Since working at the Globe, I've considered these questions quite a lot. I now think of the audience very much as people in the play, of whom you might be asking advice, or telling them what you're up to; in fact their role and nature can change quite a lot over the course of a play. In *Richard III*, for example, I found the audience was kind of on Richard's side: laughing away, almost willing him on. Then things get really weird and nasty, and suddenly you can feel that the audience starts to change, and they are not quite so much on his side anymore. The audiences tended to feel increasingly accusatory and judgemental as the play went on, which was useful for me, as Richard became more belligerent in responding to them. Then he has a scene where he loses his mind and wakes up, suddenly aware of what he's done ... responding to pricks of conscience, which (I think) are the audience ... at that point he is alone, and afraid, and aware of all these faces looking at him, accusing him.

I found playing Macbeth a very different case, because right from the offset he is aware that what he's doing is wrong; he turns to the audience and admits, 'This is bad, this is wrong, this is not going to be good.' Then, Lady M says, 'We're going to do it' ... and so then he has to deal with the audience with, 'If it were done, when 'tis done, then 'twere well / It were done quickly' (*Macbeth*, 1.7.1–28). At that moment, I found the internal dialogue I mentioned earlier was with the audience, and it went something like, 'Don't sit there and point your fingers at me accusingly, I'm a soldier. I would kill him in a flicker of an eye if I knew that I'd get away with it ... however, I don't think I will get away with it, and that's why I'm thinking I'm not going to do it.' This moment was a conversation with the audience, rather than a character making up his own mind based only on what is going on in their own head.

If you accept this idea of the audience taking a part in the play, it doesn't need to follow that the actor talks to the house all the time. There are all kinds of things you can get the audience to *do*. During a Q&A once, somebody commented on how naff she thought the idea for Birnam Wood was – just a few actors with sticks and twigs on stage; she thought this huge theatre could have made a more theatrical choice possible – and while listening I suddenly had this image of the audience themselves becoming the wood. The audience can be a place to project your ideas about your ideal future, or your worst fears; either way, they can play an important part in your character's internal dialogue.

Voice

I've picked up bits of technique along the way from various other people. I do a warm-up every time I do a show, but it hasn't changed since Jeanette Nelson at the Globe taught me a routine, which works for me, in terms of getting my voice and my body and my mind focused.

When you go to drama school, one of the biggest things that you will learn is how to retrain your body to breathe from the diaphragm. It takes a long time of doing boring, seemingly meaningless exercises day in, day out, literally to retrain your body to do it. And it's something that you risk losing connection with, even after you've gone to drama school. I know actors who left drama school, went straight into TV and then did theatre again after a few years and lost it completely.

Technically, you have to get to the point where you're not even thinking about breathing, diction or articulation, while making sure that you're hitting all of those things. The RSC help to reinforce these techniques with lots of classes and good technical support – voice and the movement stuff is all very well catered for there.

Physicality

Sometimes I have a very strong idea of how a character is supposed to look and move, and sometimes I don't. Playing Richard III, for example, I knew very early on how I wanted him to move and how I wanted him to look: very graceful, very willowy, almost balletic. So, I worked on that right from the beginning: I had heels, and a corset, which made me stand up straight to give me that height.

Macbeth was different and difficult, because I'm not necessarily a 'soldier type', so it was about finding breadth in the shoulders, planting the feet, that kind of thing. I wasn't exactly sure what that was going to be, so that was found during the rehearsals, more gradually. How it all comes together varies from job to job, of course.

The point of it all . . .

We've been talking about my process, and all of it is designed to create an experience for the audience which will move them. Ultimately, what I'm hoping for is that the sum of all that cumulative work will deliver something that's true, and hopefully if that happens, then the audience will relate to the story in some way, and will be moved.

EMILY TAAFFE, ACTOR

Character-led reading

When I read a play just for pleasure, I read it 'as a whole': reading a play for work is reading from a character's point of view, which is a very different thing. There's that joke about this, you know, when you do *The Cherry Orchard*, people might ask: 'What's it about?' and you say: 'It's about this maid called Dunyasha' because you always view the play solely through your character's eyes.

So, that would be the first thing that I would do. I would read *The Tempest*, for example, looking at it from Miranda's point of view, as in: 'Why is Prospero doing these things? Why is she being asked to go and see Caliban again? How does she feel about Prospero at the end, when he says he'll go to 'Milan, where / Every third thought shall be my grave' (*The Tempest*, 5.1.311–12)? I feel like that's my responsibility: to try it as much about my character as possible. I think every actor does that, and if everybody does that, then all the various points of view join up together, and it's the director's job to make sure that all the strands – of *music*, if you like – come together in a harmonious way, without one bit being played too loudly!

And then, I suppose, the next things I think about are the bits of the story that we *don't* see. In the example of *Twelfth Night* I might be thinking about the immediate preceding circumstances – what the storm was like – and then, beyond that, what Viola and Sebastian's home-life was like. Steven [Hagan – playing Sebastian opposite Emily's Viola] and I had talked about why they left Messaline where their mother was, and what kind of people they were: was she 'bookish' and smart? Was he the more 'blustery' sibling? That conversation usually happens in response to somebody else: Jonathan Slinger [who played Prospero] and I talked about what life on 'the island' was like; how long ago the rape happened; was it a rape? and so on. Playing Viola in the same season, I knew I was going to cut all my hair off for Viola, so for Miranda, I wondered, did she do that herself? Or did Prospero do that to de-sexualize her? You end up linking things together because you have to. And, it's a continuous process throughout the rehearsal process, because, for me, backstory and narrative are very important.

I often will write a biography of the character. When I first started working, I would begin writing that quite early on in rehearsals, but these days it happens at a later stage, because I don't want to make decisions too soon. With some of the Shakespeare plays, I'd write out my backstory, for example: what Viola had been doing the day the storm happened; what the storm was like; how she felt, because it fills in the gaps a little bit. I'll often do that for the bits between each scene that I'm in. I mean, no one in the audience will ever know I've done this, but I think the more solid you feel with the story, the more you're able to play with it.

I went to LAMDA and I remember one of the teachers saying to us: 'We are trying to give you as many colours as possible in your palette – you might only use three or four.' So I'll pick and choose different aspects of my process. With regard to building a character, I am very wary of people who sort of like crow-bar a concept onto something. If it doesn't come from something in the text it's not based on anything – it is like building castles on sand, it's never going to stay. So the techniques I use, I would say, all have some relationship to the text. For example, the next thing I do is the thing that everybody does: which is the Stanislavski thing where you study the text to find the answers to seven questions: Who am I? Where am I? What time is it? What do I want? Why do I want it? How will I get what I want? What must I overcome to get what I want? In the case of Viola this was difficult because I was playing somebody who is playing somebody else. As a result I didn't actually find the questions that useful.

When I was training we did a bit of Laban, and it can be a way in – especially if it is a character who isn't as close to your own inner tempo. So I thought about her *inner tempo* as opposed to her *outer tempo*. This proved useful for Luciana (*The Comedy of Errors*) who struck me as incredibly nervy, anxious: she'd be like an 'inner dabber' and an 'outer glider' ... she'll kind of smooth everything all the time. I didn't use Laban at all for Miranda, because I didn't feel like I needed it, but it was useful for Luciana, and if you have these techniques at your disposal you can draw on them.

Normally I'll go to galleries, in case I see things that remind me of moments in the play, or the character. I always find pieces of music that make me think of the character, and I make little playlists for each character, which I listen to before the show. I don't always listen to the same one, but I'll have a choice of about four. These have been really useful for instances when I've been cast in more than one show, when I've needed to switch between characters; in those instances you can't obsess about one character's world for six weeks, in the way you might normally. The character playlists of music are a really immediate help.

Actions

I sometimes do that 'actioning' of the text as well. I find it useful to action the text where choices can't be discovered so easily in rehearsal with a scene-partner, where you have only the audience's reactions to a soliloquy to consider, and you're on stage thinking: 'What am I trying to do?' By contrast, where I have a scene with someone, I don't make concrete decisions about 'actions' before I've had some time on my feet with my scene-partner, because I think a lot of acting is really instinctual. It's not really a formulaic thing. I think it's a conversation ... or at least it *should* be a conversation. What your scene partner brings, and what you and the director and the other actors decide you want to achieve from the scene will massively affect your choice of action. In that first scene of *The Tempest*, my instinct was to choose actions which meant I would play Miranda as a really angry 'teenager', but this was really altered because of the way Jonny [Jonathan Slinger] was playing Prospero. I think it's dangerous to make too many decisions at home on your own, as you might come into rehearsal with your own kind of ready-made plan, and that's not very much fun to play with.

Verse

Before getting cast in these shows at the RSC I'd never done Shakespeare before – I did it at drama school so that is where

I learned all about iambic pentameter. Actually, I found what I learned can be both helpful and unhelpful at points. I think it can be really good to mark the scansion out, because sometimes I wouldn't realize *that* was the important word in a line, until I'd done that. Marking out the stressed syllable can make the whole meaning of the line change slightly, and that can be really useful, and it can guide you in that way. But I also think verse-work can be a really crippling thing if you become too focused on it. I think you should know the rules, and have a look at the text with the rules, and then throw the rules away – because it's not an academic exercise, it's a living, breathing thing and I think if you become 'wedded' to *that* … you risk becoming a slave to it. I also think the fashion, the style of playing now is much more naturalistic, you want the verse to sound as if it is naturalistic speech. I think Jon Slinger does this brilliantly. Listening to him in *The Tempest* I kept thinking 'This is slightly heightened, but people understand it' … which is the most important thing. You [the actor] have to really understand it for them to understand it, and if you are worrying more about hitting beats and so religiously, it's not going to make for really good listening, I think.

I worked with some actors who just don't believe in subtext; who don't think it's important, and for them everything's about 'the line'. I remember having this full-on conversation with Gerald Kyd – who played Yasha in the same production of *The Cherry Orchard* in which I was playing Dunyasha – about whether or not they'd had sex, when we thought they might have had sex; before this particular scene or after it? I was arguing 'It can't possibly be *after* because' and Gerald was arguing: 'Well I think *this*' and Conleth [Hill, who played Lopakhin] was like: 'Who cares? The audience aren't going to know,' and I was thinking: 'Well it matters to *me* because'. But Conleth is one of the best actors I've ever worked with – phenomenal – and he just has a completely different point of view to me. And he's better than me! Surprisingly, though our processes are so different, the product isn't that dissimilar. I imagine it was ever thus, and ever will be.

YOLANDA VAZQUEZ, ACTOR AND DIRECTOR

When reading any play I tend to be led first by the story it is trying to tell, then by how the language is being used to tell that story. With Shakespeare I read it through once and immerse myself in the whole story, then I like to go back to relish specific scenes or monologues that stood out in the first reading. The very first thing I do is read it all, even if I know the play really well. If acting: I will go through it working out the metre in the scenes the character I am playing appears and underlining anything I don't understand. If directing: I go through the whole play doing the same thing.

To me what is distinctive is the way the words feel in the mouth and body, the visceral quality of it, also the pleasure of being able to express a thought or a feeling so succinctly and beautifully. The ones that come immediately to mind are 'when I love thee not / Chaos is come again' (*Othello*, 3.3.91–2), or 'I would eat his heart in the marketplace' (*Much Ado About Nothing*, 4.1.305). The challenges for me are trying to get through the linguistic gymnastics that, for a Spaniard, the conjunction of certain phrases or verse lines offer.

I'm not 100 per cent sure it does follow this particular order, it depends on my mood and on the play – but normally, as I mentioned, I read the play all the way through and get completely involved in the story. What I mean by that is that I create a vivid film of it in my mind – I read in pictures. I will then go back and read the scenes that I am involved in in more detail. I will then go through the scansion, annotating the first and last stressed syllable of each verse line and taking a moment to notice any irregularities, as well as underlining any words or areas of the text that I don't quite understand. Once I have the definition of the difficult passages/words,

I will go through the whole text for meaning, paying particular attention to the scenes I will be involved in. Once I am satisfied with the meaning, I read the scripts several times and make lists of what is said about the character and what she says of anyone else. I also like to make the same lists for any person that is closely involved with the character. This I find extremely useful and it gives me food for thought. It's fascinating to have facts about a character, rather than preconceived ideas that have come from the many versions of the play I may have seen. It's as if I am discovering the person afresh. Once I have collated this information I will think of what the Weight, Space, Time and Flow of the character might be (as in the Laban Elements) and I will take this as the starting point of what I consider the essence of the character. After this I might start to think about intentions – I allow my imagination to play with the information gathered and start to work out why this person behaves in this particular way. I might then start doing research, and read about the times and customs of that era or that country. Then I look forward to rehearsals, or this might be happening as rehearsals have just started, in order to muck about and prove everything I have just worked on to be leading me up the garden path – or not, as the case may be.

I think I still use pretty much everything I learnt in training. Maybe not as pedantically as we were taught, but I can absolutely see the seeds of my three years at Drama Centre in the homework I do. This can be described as Stanislavski via Yat Malgrem and Laban, with a pinch of Christopher Fettes. I also use large doses of Cicely Berry, Giles Block and Tim Carroll ... added to this a strong fragrance of subversion from Robert David MacDonald and Philip Prowse ... all mixed in with my own imagination!

Creatives

MIKE ALFREDS, DIRECTOR

An introduction to Shakespeare

I was an avid reader and theatregoer from a very early age but, unlike some children who instinctively find his work magical and revelatory, I found Shakespeare unreadable and performances of his plays incomprehensible. It was torture to sit there. I could hear the words but didn't have a clue what the characters were on about (more on this later). So when I embarked on a career as a director, self-preservation made me steer well clear of him. I didn't want my ignorance and stupidity displayed to the world.

I was well into my forties before I plucked up the courage to tackle him. At that time, I'd set up a company called Shared Experience with the purpose of proving that theatre could exist solely with the presence of actors and audience together at the same time in the same place (not necessarily a theatre) with some sort of material to perform without any recourse to design or technology: human beings in a shared but empty space. The actors could – and indeed did – provide everything that was necessary for a complete theatrical experience. We told stories, adapted non-dramatic texts, improvised and devised material and deliberately kept away from plays. We were afraid plays might tempt us to fall back on old habits, a bit of scenery, a bit of lighting ... But after four years, it seemed time to bite the bullet and apply the new skills and insights we'd accumulated to a proper dramatic text. And because of our austerity of means, Shakespeare seemed the appropriate playwright (open stage, natural light).

So I set out to read the canon. Perversely, I started with one of the least-known plays. *Cymbeline* at this time was rarely performed. The general view of it was of a long and lumpy play with incompatible elements. From the first scene I fell for it. It made total sense to me, and its different worlds (Ancient Britain, Renaissance Italy and Imperial Rome) didn't seem the least bit incompatible. Five actors played all the roles and we had twelve weeks' rehearsal. Those were the days! It was a joyful voyage of discovery and, encouragingly, a success. Next came *The Merchant of Venice*. I had noticed an unexpected similarity between the characters and plots of that play and those of the *commedia dell'arte*, a form of theatre I'd studied, worked on and loved. Shylock was a *Pantalone*, the comic villain; Portia and Bassanio were the well-bred *Innamorati*; Lancelot Gobbo was an *Arlecchino*; the Prince of Morocco was a *Capitano*. The story of the miserly father whose daughter or young wife steals his money and runs away from him was one of the motifs of *commedia* scenarios. So, I decided to do the play with the actors masked as characters from that world. At the start, the two disciplines (*commedia* masks and Shakespearian verse) seemed irreconcilable. But, eventually, when we were touring to a festival in Toronto, the two elements successfully coalesced. Since then, I've done nine of his plays, some of them more than once. Nevertheless, whenever I set off on a Shakespeare text, there is still that lurking anxiety that some academic is going to announce to the world that Mike Alfreds is an analphabet who shouldn't be allowed anywhere near the greatest works in our national heritage.

The text

For me, the irony of working on Shakespeare is that the language which I'd found so impenetrable years ago is, of course, the fount and basis of the work from which all else springs. This, of course, should be true of any piece of literature. *How* a story is told, that is, how language is deployed to tell any story, is what gives it its identity, its logic, its specificity, its thematic resonances, its particular world ... its life. Character, plot and theme come second.

This emphasis on language, I hasten to stress, does *not* imply some misconceived idea of poetic delivery. Verse is not necessarily poetry. There are still actors around who believe it is their duty to express the beauty of the text. It isn't. Their job is to convey the thoughts, feelings, intentions and actions of their character. The emphasis on language means, for me, first of all looking closely at *how the words are put on the page*: their sequence, their position in a verse line, their sound (assonance, consonance alliteration, onomatopoeia), their length (syllabic count), the multiple associations of their meaning (puns), their rhythmic variation within the pulse of the iambic pentameter ... By analysing the structure of the words, by reverse engineering, you begin to discover the thoughts that bring them into existence.

Shakespeare didn't write stage directions, but they are implicit in the way he organized his words. As a simple example, a speech heavy in consonants and constructed mostly of words of one syllable implicitly instructs the actor to slow down. Conversely, words that are consonant-light and multisyllabic suggest they can be spoken 'trippingly'. A change of rhythm midway through a verse line could suggest a sudden change of thought, a moment of uncertainty ... Hidden instructions like these guide us towards the possible motives and attitudes of the speakers, which is why, of all writers, performing Shakespeare in a foreign language seems more or less pointless. You get the characters, plot and themes, but you're deprived of the instructions: Shakespeare's infinitely subtle deployment of the English language gives specific meaning and resonance to what is being played. There are virtually no one-to-one correspondences between languages. Something is always lost or added. *Traduttori traditori* (translators are traitors).

Performance

I described the torture of going to Shakespeare as a child. Unfortunately, that experience has persisted, relentlessly, year after year, into old age. But now that I've learnt better – that it's not because of the language – I can only put the cause of my boredom down to the actors who deliver it. So, I'll make two sweeping statements. The first is that many, if not most, actors playing Shakespeare don't really know what they're talking about. Their understanding of their texts is approximate, undetailed and unspecific. The second – and a possible reason for the first – is that when they speak, there is little sign of them thinking; that's to say, they are not going through any thought process that would give rise to the words they are speaking. To be believable, which they are not, their words should be spontaneous utterances that only they could say at that moment. The actors have forged no relationship with the text. They have failed to make Shakespeare's language their own.

This is bad acting. The causes are numerous: inadequate techniques, lack of experience and insufficient time to deal with the unfamiliarity of the language, not only the obscure vocabulary or familiar-looking words that now mean the opposite of what they once did, but also the lengthy thought sequences, the grammar-defying sentence structures, the imagery … and, not least, directors, so bent on imposing their concepts of *Lear* onto *Lear*, and focusing on those elements of the production that will show off the relevance of their interpretations, that language is often the last thing to be dealt with. It should be the first. The ideas for a production and its performance have to come *out* of the language, not be put *on* it.

Now I've got that off my chest, I have some observations of how and why blocks to comprehension occur, and possible suggestions to overcome them.

Conversations

Shakespeare writes plays just as most other playwrights write plays. He tells his stories mainly through dialogue. But because his language is heightened and his plays come burdened with a lot of received ideas, some actors have come to treat their speeches, especially the longer ones, as sealed-off, self-contained units provided for the expression of their feelings and characterization. That's all very well and good, but whatever the characters are saying – however emotionally charged, intellectually complex and imagery rich – they are nonetheless having conversations. A speech is usually the reaction to another speech; what Character A has said elicits a response from Character B. Embedded within a speech will be certain words or phrases that pick out and refer directly back to words or phrases embedded in previous speeches, synonymous or antonymous word or phrases that make us understand that a conversation is taking place. And I, the audience, have to hear that conversation, hear those words bouncing off each other. I have to hear characters talking *to* each other, rather than emoting *in front of* each other. I may hear the words, but if I don't hear the conversational logic, I will have no idea what is going on. I won't follow the story. Therefore it would be wise for actors, first and foremost, to understand – and make their own – the common-sense, bottom-line, interpretation-free, emotion-free, utterly logical journey of their dialogue before they worry about anything else: the motivation, characterization, situation, emotional state.

Living through the language

Shakespeare's characters live through language. They live on the word. Their language is elaborate, complicated, rich in metaphors, puns and the like. This is their predominant means of expression; they live – shall we say 80 or 90 per cent of their lives? – through language. This is because in the reality of Shakespeare's worlds, the characters are verbally sophisticated and wish to convey precisely, meticulously, what they want other characters to understand. Their images, similes and the like are not mere decorative devices on the part of a self-indulgent playwright, but the specific choices made by characters determined to communicate exactly, *exactly*, how they feel or what they think. (We'll discuss the final image in the speech of Imogen, in a moment.) For them language is tangible; it is sensuous, fleshy, corporeal. They use it as a weapon, a scalpel, an embrace.

Because of this determination to be understood, there is virtually no subtext. Characters say what they mean. If they are going to lie, they warn us in advance. All this is particularly true of the verse which comes directly from the heart. After all, an iamb is a heartbeat: ba-boom, ba-boom, ba-boom, ba-boom.

The prose is another matter. Characters use prose to cover what they really intend: when they are not meaning what they say, or saying what they mean, or are not quite sure how they feel, when they are functioning through indirection, or when they are so foolish that they don't know what they're talking about or understand what is being said to them. Shakespeare's clowns and fools all speak in prose. The prose can often be far more clotted, trickier to catch than the verse. Puns and plays on words are more frequent (check the exchanges between Beatrice and Benedick in *Much Ado About Nothing*). The ratio of verse to prose in a play will give you some idea of what the play is about and at what levels the characters function. In *Twelfth Night*, Malvolio speaks prose up to the final scene when he switches to verse.

Actors are often shy of committing themselves to the convention of rhymed couplets and find ways to avoid them, throwing them away, letting them fade or totally destroying the couplet's rhythm. But rhymes have a purpose. Characters use them because they need them, maybe to consolidate a statement or score a point, clinch a deal or because they want to bring a situation to its close … Actors have to find a motivation that will allow us to hear the rhyme and totally understand their reason for using it, accepting it as a natural part of the world they are inhabiting.

Shouting in lieu of feeling

My experience at most productions of Shakespeare is that an awful lot of shouting goes on, shouting that is neither expressive nor revelatory nor necessary. I suppose the heightened nature of the language and the passionate nature of the events are signals to the actors that something more than contemporary naturalism is required. But because of the lack of textual understanding or thought process I mentioned earlier, the actors have been unable to create an authentic dramatic existence that would allow them access to any true feeling. They remain in their heads and out of their bodies. Therefore, all they can do is substitute tension for intensity, and generalized anger for genuine emotion. Shouting – playing 'angry' – is the easy and inadequate mode actors often resort to as a way of demonstrating intense feeling in the absence or avoidance of the real thing. This blunts and flattens the text: everything sounds the same.

Lost words, false endings and sustained thoughts

Some actors try to solve the problem of handling a long speech, with its subtle arguments and multiple clauses, by

rushing through it before (they fear) it flies out of their
control. That only compounds the problem. They put a lot
of attack into the beginning of a verse line or phrase, but
before they've completed it, they'll be anticipating and
rushing headlong into the next. So, the end of one phrase
tends to blur into the start of the next one, and the thought
contained in it is left incomplete and unclear. And though the
audience can probably hear the words, they may feel they
haven't really understood what's been said and therefore
what is happening. It's essential that the action conveying a
thought should be sustained right through to its last syllable
and beyond; an action carries on even after the words are
over. This sense of inaudibility is not a matter of volume, it is
a matter of intention. If the thought is there, the words will
be heard. This droop is noticeable when a speech contains a
lot of end-stopped lines.

Delivering or listening to such speeches is not part of
our contemporary reality. We live in an age of sound bites,
abbreviations and acronyms. We're becoming less and less
used to sustaining extended thoughts either in our heads, in
our hearing or in our speech. So actors have to relearn a skill
that's more or less atrophied from desuetude: how to sustain
long speeches and complex thoughts.

We've dealt with endings that aren't fulfilled. Now we're
presented with the problem of non-endings treated as if they
were endings. A firm downward inflection (autonomically
accompanied by an exhalation of breath) is usually a signal
to the listener that a thought has been completed (we quite
naturally take a new breath with every new thought). If
a sentence with a sustained thought is constructed on an
elaborate sequence of multiple and qualifying clauses (we can
use Imogen's speech as an example of this), the actor has to
keep all those clauses, like juggled balls, up in the air until
the thought has been completed, at which time all the balls
can be caught and brought to rest. Some actors, whenever

they reach a comma, a dash or the end of a verse line, either
fade or let their inflection droop (dropping the ball) or make a
firmly stressed downward inflection (bringing the ball to rest),
causing a premature and false completion. The full thought will
be fragmented into aurally disconnected phrases, each maybe
intelligible in itself, but sequentially making little sense to an
audience. Audiences, hearing a firm downward inflection, will
assume the thought is at an end and are likely to take a brief
pause in their listening. But if the thought actually continues,
they're caught napping and have to run to catch up, and so
they miss the first two or three words of the new phrase or
thought.

IMOGEN
Ere I could tell him
How I would think on him at certain hours,
Such thoughts, and such: or I could make him swear
The shes of Italy should not beray
Mine interest, and his honour; or have charg'd him,
At the sixth hour of morn, at noon, at midnight,
T'encounter me with orisons, for then
I am in heaven for him; or ere I could
Give him that parting kiss, which I had set
Betwixt two charming words, comes in my father,
And like the tyrannous breathing of the north,
Shakes all our buds from growing.
                              (*Cymbeline*, 1.3.27–37)

In Imogen's speech – which also happens to be one sentence –
to a loyal servant, she laments her father's disruption of
the leave-taking she'd been preparing for her husband,
Posthumus, whom he has banished. The sentence's pay-off
comes in the last two-and-a-half lines, but the actor has first
to get through all the details in the clauses and phrases of the
nine preceding verse lines before she can fulfil the thought

that's motivating the sentence. The simple bare bones of this
sentence are:

> Ere I could tell him how I would think on him,
> comes in my father and shakes all our buds from
>   growing.

She has to sustain the thought through all of the speech's
twelve lines with its many detailed clauses. If the drive of the
speech gets lost and breaks down into discrete fragments, this
is what happens:

> Ere I could tell him how I would think on him at certain
>   hours. [*drop/rest*]
> Such thoughts and such. [*drop/rest*]
> Or I could make him swear the shes of Italy should not
>   betray mine interest and his honour. [*drop/rest*]
> Or have charged him at the sixth hour of morn, at noon,
>   at midnight t'encounter me with orisons. [*drop/rest*]
> For then I am in heaven for him. [*drop/rest*]
> Or ere I could give him that parting kiss. [*drop/rest*]
> Which I had set betwixt two charming words. [*drop/
>   rest*]
> Comes in my father. [*drop/rest*]
> And like the tyrannous breathing of the north. [*drop/
>   rest*]
> Shakes all our buds from growing. [*drop/rest*]

This is unbearable – in fact impossible – to listen to.

Because the point of this speech-sentence-thought comes
in the last two-and-a-half lines, the character clearly knows
what she wants to say ('Listen to how my father destroyed
everything I'd planned as a loving farewell'), so it's for the
actor to commit to the character's need to share her loss with
her servant's sympathetic ear. Then the prolixity of the speech
shouldn't present a problem. As long as the overall intention
of the sentence is sustained, the actor can take her time,

communicating clearly and specifically each of the individual thoughts along the way because she knows where she's heading.

Incidentally, the last two lines, a simile and a metaphor, are good examples of the dramatic use of such devices. They are in no way fanciful decoration. They are concrete images that sum up everything Imogen has been saying. They could hardly be more appropriate.

To cut or not to cut

Shakespeare's plays are for the most part too long for our impatient era. The common practice is to make them shorter.

One of the facts that helped me to engage with Shakespeare was the discovery that those of his texts that have come down to us are by no means sacrosanct Ur-versions. Some plays, as we know, exist both in folio and quarto. We also know that the plays were not exclusively performed at the Globe or Blackfriars, but also in Royal Palaces and on tour around the country. Cuts may well have been made to accommodate the performance needs of different venues. It's also possible that the plays were never completely finished in Shakespeare's mind and he may have used revivals to refine or elaborate what he had already written or to suit the abilities of a replacement actor; after all, he was a practical man working with and for a specific company in special circumstances. There are clear indications that his clowns may have improvised their own parts and when we read their speeches we may be reading Kemp's and Armin's jokes rather than Shakespeare's. The 'parts' – texts given to the actors with just their lines and cues on them – were, of course, copied by hand, possibly from originals that were in places illegible and therefore dependent on educated guesses. Some speeches may have been written down from memory. So there's every reason to believe that those scribes caused occasional omissions or additions, as well as the misplacement of lines, speeches, even scenes … Some verse lines are unusually short, lacking their full five iambs or, conversely, they have more than the regulation ten syllables. Are these copiers' mistakes or Shakespeare's intended stage directions? It seems we really have no idea exactly what he wrote! The fully played version of *Hamlet* is some four hours long, double the often quoted 'two hours' traffic of our stage' (*Romeo and Juliet*, Prologue.12). But this version could possibly be a conflation from several different performances put together for the Folio edition printed seven years after his death. Maybe the intention was to make his work available to the reader rather than the performer. All this suggests that the plays that have come down to us are versions of constantly developing, living-and-breathing organisms, flexible and porous enough to let in lots of fresh air.

But this shouldn't be taken as permission or an inducement to do any old thing you like with those texts. Cuts should never be made merely as a contingency, nor from laziness when confronted by dense chunks of obscurity; nor to get rid of lines that would contradict your interpretation of the play. Instead, you grapple with every part of the text for its verbal meaning, its purpose in the scene, its revelation of character and motivation, its clarification of story and plot ... Otherwise, a lot of hacking takes place and the baby gets thrown out with the bath water.

Iambic pentameters

Most of the plays are mostly in verse. As Shakespeare also wrote in prose, it is obvious that he intended a different purpose for each of them, suggestions for which I've already made. Therefore, it's lazy and reductive to treat verse as if it were prose. The verse has an energy that demands its speakers function at a heightened level of existence. Attempts to make the language sound natural by a sort of casual delivery remove its passion and its drive. The actor's job should be to convince us that a heightened form of speaking is utterly natural. The characters can speak in no other way!

Ignoring the verse can also distort the meaning of the text. A change of rhythm within an iambic pentameter, say, is one of those implicit stage directions that might suggest a change of thought, a moment of self-doubt, a loss of temper … Also, it's important to know which word takes the stress within a verse line (there's only one per line) because it clarifies the line's meaning. That stress can land on any of the five strong beats. Often the stressed word seems counterintuitive. In Imogen's speech the stressed words, line by line are: *Ere, How*, the second *such, not, charged, mid*night, *then, him, set, fa*ther, *ty*rannous, *all*. The variation in the position of the stress produces a constant liveliness.

Conversely, mindless slavery to a misconception about the verse line can give rise to an unnatural metronomic beat. Don't be afraid of the iambic pentameter. It is simply a pulse – as I said, a heartbeat – repeated five times, providing ten alternating weak and strong syllables. What's more, it's the natural pulse of the English language; we speak in iambic pentameters all day long: *I'd love a cup of coffee if you're buying. I haven't heard a nightingale in years.*

From play to play Shakespeare experimented with language, trying to get closer to the way people actually thought and spoke. In early plays like *Richard III* the verse lines have regular end-stops, very much the practice of the time. By his final plays they are running-on freely, often with more syllables than the official ten. These additional beats have to be accommodated within the pentameter. It has become something of a cliché to see Shakespearean verse as form of jazz, but it's still worth pointing out the analogy. You can construct endless variations of rhythm and tempo upon the ground bass of the iambic pentameter.

Working on Shakespeare requires immense rigour. Only through discipline can actors achieve any creative freedom. Approximation and generalization are deadly. Accuracy and specificity lead to life. It is there within these texts, waiting to be released.

TIM CARROLL, DIRECTOR

Ways of reading Shakespeare

My first step when coming to work on a Shakespeare play is to try to imagine it as it would have been played in Shakespeare's own time. That's the best way for me to try and clear my head of all of the productions I've seen. Indeed, I'm someone who has experimented with 'original practices', and found a lot of pleasure in doing that. One of the reasons I have found that so thrilling is because as soon as you start to work with 'original practices', you realize that nobody *does* do this: this is not the same as deciding, 'Well, let's do it in Elizabethan costumes.' If you *really* tell yourself: 'Here we are in the Globe, which looks as much like the Globe as we can make it look, and therefore we *could* do a show that is as much like the first performance as we can make it, *if* we were to do *that*, how would it go?' the beauty of that approach is that you find yourself picturing something completely different from any version of the play you've ever seen.

It is more to do with solving a practical problem. I don't think of 'cool images' or 'cool effects'. Even if I am not working in the Globe for this particular production, I go straight to the question of the space, because it gives me a kind of ground-base against which to measure and justify every change. I like the practical questions, such as 'is that bit of the play an upper level bit, and if so, does it mean it should be in the musicians' gallery? In which case, how can you get the actor from there, to their next entrance, which is coming along very soon?' When I understand the play in terms of those practical questions, then I feel like I am getting quite close to 'an event'; as soon as I am reading a play I want to be thinking in terms of 'events'.

If you are a director, it is refreshing to read the work of academics, because they *haven't* been coming from the same place you have, and because they have been able to imagine things in a very irresponsible way, and it's nice to read those things. It allows you to notice these connections between ideas because maybe you haven't noticed those connections before, because you have been so busy thinking, 'Can I get all those people on stage in the space of those two lines?', or whatever. It is important that we respect the separation of being a director of Shakespeare and of writing literary criticism of Shakespeare. I challenge the assumption that literary critics of Shakespeare *need* to take performance into account more. You can of course *read* a play like *Richard III* – and it is a beautiful thing to read – though it was of course written for the theatre, and that is no doubt part of its essential nature. But as for those critics who, as it were, point out connections between something on page 1 and page 100, which would not be noticeable in the theatre … that doesn't mean that connection isn't there, it just means that you are a chump if, in the theatre as a director, you try to bring that out. I like reading Jan Kott's *Shakespeare Our Contemporary* (1974) or Northrop Frye's essays on Shakespeare (1986), which I find inspiring, but I don't know how these feed into my work. If I knew, the work wouldn't be good.

Cutting and casting

The two most practical and crucial bits of pre-rehearsal preparation are the cutting and the casting of the piece. I will read the play several times to work out problems of cutting and casting, deciding whether a line earns its place or not. Even if I end up not cutting anything, I read with a much better attention when I'm trying to decide what to cut and *if* to cut. When you are looking for cuts, it really makes you think about what every bit of the play is doing, and why it needs to be there. Within my cut, I like to prepare my own acting edition, and I tend to start from the First Folio. I often find that I go back to the more problematic reading that subsequent editors have changed, on the principle of *lectio difficilior potior* – as we used to say in Classics – the more difficult reading should stand.

In terms of casting, there are two ways in which that's very focusing. One of them is the question of how many actors you need, which forces you to think about the practicalities of how many people are on stage, and which characters are never on stage together and so on, all of which gets you even more familiar with the play. And there is also the question of thinking about a particular actor, and thinking that 'he might be very good for such a part' and then going back through the play and thinking, 'Can I see that, is that what I really want?' All of that really helps me.

Verse and other games with rules

I quite like the question 'To what tradition do you belong?', because everything belongs to some sort of tradition, even if you think you've invented it. So the simple answer, which is actually slightly misleading, is that it's a mixture of the Peter Hall tradition and the Peter Brook tradition. That pretty much sums it up – in the same sense that Peter Hall is in the Dadie Rylands tradition and Peter Brook is in the Artaud tradition (and others). I would say I'm sort of fusing those two, because the verse work is very fascistic, increasingly rigorous, and the rehearsal exercises are more and more about spontaneity, and playfulness.

'Play' is the word, that's the whole point, and actually the strictness of the rules helps you play, because it makes the play more fun. The more of those rules you add, the more interesting the game gets. So it all comes down to play, because in the performance itself, we don't get hung up on the 'suspension of disbelief' idea, which people would associate with Stanislavski ... though I bet they wouldn't if they saw his productions. We don't get hung up on the idea that we must create a mood where everyone is able, somehow, to believe that he happens to be thinking out loud and we're not really here ... all of that seems to be mental effort wasted. So, by simply saying 'right, here we are to play the game of *Hamlet*', we allow the kind of emotional engagement to arise informally, if you like, or almost accidentally. I think that is the only way that emotional engagement *can* arise. That, rather than try to transmit a mood or emotion to the audience, we simply start responding, in the same way that musicians might rehearse in a sort of jamming way, I suppose.

The game of 'can I be responsive to what you do?' and the game of 'can I do that without buggering the verse?' are in the same part of me, as I play. They both happen simultaneously. I use the language of clowning and improvisation in my notes, a lot. I often say, for instance, 'Did you not see that he was making you an offer?', to which the answer will either be 'Yes I did, but I was too cowardly to accept it, sorry', or 'Oh, I see, oh, I thought he was trying to do *that*, oh, what an idiot', or 'No, I didn't see it at all.' But that language of improvisation is very important in this kind of work. Because it *is* a kind of improvisation.

One also uses the language of an even-more-rigorous Peter Hall, for example, 'You stressed that word. Is that word in the stressed position? No? Well, then, why did you stress it? We don't do that.' Not a line reading, but a line instruction. I don't say anything about volume, pitch, speed, attitude, intention. Given that those are all still available to you, there are still about seventy-six million things you can do with every line, if you just take what I'm saying about ictus. Just say it in the right rhythm for me, and then do whatever you like with it.

I suppose my three rules for rehearsal are simple:

1. We mustn't ever go too long without practising verse, like doing scales.

2. We mustn't ever go too long without checking that we know what the language means.

3. We mustn't ever go too long without talking about actions.

In terms of time management, my rehearsals would have an hour on language, an hour on actions and an hour on verse. Things must, however, happen in a correct order of discovery, as it were. I try not to work heavily on understanding the language until I've done quite a lot of verse. Partly because I had a very interesting correspondence with Tom Clayton at the University of Minnesota. He read David Crystal's book *Pronouncing Shakespeare* (2005) and he read my introduction to it and liked what I said about using the verse, to find out how they would have spoken it. He wrote that if you try to puzzle out what it means, before you scan it, then you get it wrong, and then you scan it wrong. Whereas, if you try to scan it first, then it tells you what it means, and you get to the meaning much quicker. So we don't talk about the meaning of it for about the first two weeks of rehearsal; instead we would spend the first two weeks making sure we could *say* it all metrically. By that time, people have worked out what it means, because they're scanning it right.

I do sometimes get actors to paraphrase the text into their own words, but that is at a later stage. If you spend the first couple of weeks thrashing out 'what it means', you could get half of that wrong, and then of course the danger is that you then decide, 'Oh, that must be interesting off-beat', for example [stresses in bold], 'I would **not** have **you** come **here**', instead of 'I **would** not **have** you **come** here'. So you've just made everything clotted for yourself, and Shakespeare suddenly feels very *sturm und drang* … lots of barnstorming bombast, whereas I think Shakespeare is actually lighter, and subtler. It's not at all *without* emotion, but that emotion is sublimated in the verse.

I was interested in verse before I was interested in directing. It is probably true to say that I was interested in verse before I was interested in theatre. My father was a poet, and from him, I've always had a great passion for poetry and great interest in verse. I remember, in 1984, John Barton's series *Playing Shakespeare* was on TV, and I was watching it with my dad. And I was shouting at the TV when Richard Pasco kept getting it wrong. And my father said, 'You've obviously got a good ear for this, because I can't hear the difference', and I got really obsessed with that series. I got the book, and it became my bible for a bit, which is interesting because now I don't agree with most of it! I agree absolutely with the things Barton knows, but I actually now don't agree with how he applies it. But that's fine, I still admire him enormously. It was through that book, and through wanting to put that stuff into practice, that I got into directing.

The Factory's *Hamlet*

I thought to myself, 'Well, I love the idea of *Different Every Night* (Alfreds, 2014), but what we need is a set-up which leaves the actors no choice but to do it differently.' We're never 'generating difference' for the sake of it, we are simply responding to different 'givens' every night. That's why we change the cast, change the venue whenever possible and ask the audience to bring the objects we'll play with. We cast it by lottery: actors play 'rock, paper, scissors' in pairs. This way of working provides its own challenges: because nobody's paid, it is all about who happens to have a free evening, so the size of the company can vary on any given night, depending on who's available. All of the actors have learned at least two parts, several of them have learnt seven or eight parts. That means that even if lots of people are not available, we almost certainly have got everything covered, and we've always got a different cast every time we play it.

In terms of rehearsal, we just do exercises. It's much more like training. We train to be good at doing verse, to be good at responding to each other's offers. We train to have strong voices, to have good spatial awareness, to be physically fit and flexible. Everyone does it because they want to do it. I said at our first session, 'Because we aren't paying anyone, nobody must do anything they don't want to. I will *never* do anything for you simply because you came to so many sessions – you create no obligation in me. And I will never put in an invoice to you for all the training you get from me. We are all here tonight because we want to be here tonight.' We start work at seven on the dot, we go through to ten, we don't break for coffee or anything and we always work intensely.

We don't discuss collectively agreed units of the play. The whole point of The Factory is to agree on as little as possible, because I want everyone to be in their own element. In order to keep every possible version of *Hamlet* in the game, it is important that everyone has their view about what is happening. The only thing I think we need to agree on – apart from that we will do verse – is what the words mean. And then, what each actor means by it is up to them, but ideally, isn't up to them to decide *now*, but it is up to them to choose in the moment of performance.

Your objectives as a director naturally change over time. There isn't one set of objectives for working on Shakespeare. When I directed *Twelfth Night*, my objective was to make the 'purest' original practices thing I could make, because original practices save you all the time that you would otherwise spend trying to work out how to make an equivalent of yellow stockings, or how to make an equivalent of cross-gartering, because you *have* yellow stockings, cross-gartered. The enormous simplicity of that means you can get onto the play very quickly. And whereas I had a kind of idealized production in mind for *Twelfth Night* which I strove towards, the whole point with *Hamlet* is that there *is* no ideal production. There is no stable production at all. Therefore, the goal is to get better and better at playing whatever happens on that night, in whatever space, with whatever cast, with whatever objects the audience have brought with them. When The Factory played *Hamlet* in Kingston (11–16 April 2001) I felt that the company was beginning to bear fruit, in terms of its facility with the verse, its freedom of interpretation and its willingness to let the scene be different things, in a way that no other company's work could. I think the way The Factory works may be unique.

BUNNY CHRISTIE, DESIGNER

The best thing about working on a Shakespeare play is generally how free you can be. He leaves a lot of scope to find contemporary links or metaphors so that the plays can stay relevant and vivid. I think in the United Kingdom we can happily be quite irreverent with his work in the way that Russians can be with Chekhov. Generally, when starting on a Shakespeare production, everything is up for grabs in a way that wouldn't be the case with a production of a Pinter play, or a Beckett play, or most contemporary new plays, which are located in particular worlds. This also means it's easy to design, say, *Hamlet* or *A Midsummer Night's Dream* several times over and not repeat a process or ideas.

Studying the script, being able to analyse and figure out the language and plot detail is particularly important in Shakespeare. Though the style of language doesn't make a specific difference to my process, what's being said obviously does, and Shakespeare's breadth of images and atmospheres are exciting and inspiring for a designer. It's useful to have seen other productions: more than is the case for most other writers, Shakespeare's plays shine in performance in a way they don't on the page. Some knowledge of the politics or history involved can also be useful.

I read and reread the piece, and after that I do a detailed breakdown of the script. For each scene, I note who is present, where it is, what time of day it is and what the action of the scene is. I also make a grid in my notebook for every scene, containing notes on any special visual moments, sounds, atmosphere, costume or quick changes required, and any special effects, tricks or other thoughts I have about the scene.

Then I will talk to the director, and we may decide the world we are interested in, and what era we want to set the play in. Often that's contemporary. I will then come up with visual references, including photos, paintings, stuff from magazines, images I find online, adverts, films, scribbles in my notebook … whatever has a feeling or mood, a taste, a smell, a feeling of the production.

After that, I will begin to create a shape in the theatre or wherever we are working, starting with rough white card model using shapes of spaces working accurately to scale. This is gradually worked up. Often the main practical concern is how to get from scene to scene, that is, making the show flow, and orchestrating the whole evening.

Well before the rehearsals begin, the director and I will meet once a week, during which time I keep refining and developing the design through to the final model. Over the same period of time I meet with the production manager to make sure of the build requirements and the budget. And I'm also talking to the lighting designer and sound designer to incorporate these elements into the work.

Once rehearsals begin I'm checking on the build, doing fittings, checking on props, watching rehearsals. Often I'm reminding the director of ideas we had, or incorporating new ideas from rehearsals into the orchestration of the production. I see the role of the designer to be a production designer, leading on the whole visual look and effect of the piece. So while I am designing the show I am imagining the finished feel and atmosphere of the production. Once we get into tech I have to key back into those feelings and try to steer the production so it replicates those atmospheres. This is often most obvious in scene changes where the lighting, the sound and the scenery have to be orchestrated to match or punctuate the actors movements or words. It's like film editing, so that at times the production might need a full stop at the end of scene to jump cut to the next, or it might need underscoring so that one scene melts in to the next. If there are moving pieces of set or scene changes, then how the atmosphere shifts and what the audience is being told to look at is very important. None of this is particular to working on Shakespeare. This is how I work on any play.

I don't see my work as belonging to a particular tradition, but Philip Prowse was a big influence when I was starting out. More latterly, I've been influenced by and drawn to the work of Vicki Mortimer and Katie Mitchell, Robert Lepage, Gregory Crewdson, Ivo Van Hove, Es Devlin, Michael Levine, Thomas Ostermeir, James Turrell and Pina Bausch.

GERALDINE COLLINGE, DIRECTOR OF EVENTS AND EXHIBITIONS, RSC

My job at the RSC is about change: changing the artists, audiences and communities the RSC welcomes and works with. I have to think about the offers we make to different sections of the public, how we encourage them into the building and how we develop that audience. My team and I work with different artists and makers, who respond to different plays by making exhibitions, installations, events and other ways of animating the building to create a bigger offer. I was lucky in being able to recruit an amazing team of outward-facing individuals who are excited about Shakespeare without being too rooted in the history of the RSC or in traditional ways of thinking about Shakespeare.

The challenge and the delight of my job is that my team has to operate on very different levels all at the same time. A question for my team is: what does it mean for Stratford, a small market town in the middle of Warwickshire, to have a building such as the RSC, which would be more commonplace in London? I consider it part of my job to make sure that the RSC belongs at the heart of the town, that it belongs to the people of this region, as well as having a national and international profile.

We have to consider what we offer to local children, as much as to American tourists, or to international actors and directors, for example.

Artists are excited to respond to Shakespeare, and so it isn't difficult to find coherence in events planning. Taking different artists around this vast building, while discussing with them what they might be inspired by, it is very helpful to have Shakespeare as a kind of anchorpoint. A lot of the work I do involves considering the place that Shakespeare has here, and the space Shakespeare occupies, in the broadest sense. We have to consider how we relate to Shakespeare in the building, in this space, and how, for example, the thrust stage changed our relationship to the work. In my job, I use the thrust stage, as well as the online digital relationship with Shakespeare, as metaphors for that process of breaking down traditional barriers, bringing people closer to Shakespeare, changing people's perceptions of Shakespeare and changing their relationship to Shakespeare.

I was brought in to 'explore and explode' the work of the RSC, and so it has been important to remain playful in responding to the plays, and not to be too reverent, always. It's part of my job to make sure that the plays are as accessible as possible to as many different sections of the community.

As part of the Artistic Planning team, my job involves collaboration with other departments, for example, Education. But where my job differs from, say, Jacqui O'Hanlon's [RSC director of education] is that mine is artist-driven, commercially-driven and access-driven. It's about change, as I've said, and this includes changes in the kind of artists we are commissioning at the RSC. This will ultimately influence the work on stage, so there's more to the agenda than access.

Of course there is a big digital element to my work too. Using different vehicles – for example, the 2012 World Shakespeare Festival – we have opportunities to do big participatory, digital projects which are challenging and exciting and which we hope will change the way people think about the RSC and change the way they think about Shakespeare.

It's not just about being outward-facing either, it is about changing from within. Part of my job is to connect the artists and companies we commission work from, into the organization itself, to disrupt things, if you will. Looking back, to things like 'Such Tweet Sorrow', though I wasn't completely happy with it, I can see how that affected a big brand-change. It represented a big shift in what people expected of the RSC. The RSC's history has been for the most part shaped by a succession of famous artistic directors; I want to do more projects like Open Stages, which changed the relationship with a particular community, one which spans the country, and which has challenged, and to an extent changed, who we think of as the makers of RSC work.

MICHAEL CORBIDGE, VOICE COACH

When I first meet a group of actors it's usually at the first read through as a company. I find read-throughs to be quite sedentary affairs, I'm not a great believer in sitting down, mumbling or mouthing the words. Shakespeare is such a 'doing' occupation and it requires you to be in a mode of doing-ness! So, standing up and moving in the space and allowing that motion to start lifting the text off the page and launching it into said space … it's a very early stage but an important one to see the body-voice connection, and often those first decisions those actors make are really instinctive and intuitive.

My job is to get a first impression and see what's going on for each actor. It's my first contact with them and important, because over the coming weeks I have to create a sort of file on each one of them. Now, what I mean by file is I look at their physicality, analyse how they're making sounds and make judgements about what they are doing. Various things get thrown up, and they're not always negative and not always massive issues either. Often a few tweaks, sharing of ideas and working a drill and building a secure regime are what's needed. I might pick up on an actor's nasality, having weak S's, or restricted breath flow; I'm looking at speech faults, essentially, the knowledge of which helps me to work specifically on an actor's voice, colouring the tone, expanding the note range or reducing tension. That's where my work begins, but that amount of detail is something I have to keep going all the way through the rehearsal process, through previews, to press night and beyond. Even once the show is underway my work doesn't stop, because the integrity of the director's vision and all the other artistic input has to be kept up. Also, the psychology of every actor is different so it's important for me to know how some issues will peel and shift over time, where it's low priority and when I need to start sharing it as a higher priority.

Some rehearsal rooms honour the voice and text support, welcoming it and using it. Voice and text support forms an integrated part of the process of play building, so rehearsals represent a rich, ripe time to work with directors, and they allow us to work with actors in solo calls, pairs or in small groups. We are also an active support mechanism in the rehearsal room, collaborating and building with the director. It can also take the form of dedicated time on the stage, and some fine-tuning work across tech days, in previews, and of course beyond opening night.

One thing I'm very passionate about is vocal health and safety. Safe voicing is at the top of my agenda! Rehearsals are lengthy, tiring and often pressurized affairs, so my job is to keep everybody safe and keep an ear and eye out for issues of vocal mis-management. I simply call it my 'Management, Maintenance and Hygiene of the Voice Kit'! It's exactly like doing a course in car maintenance, for your voice. I make actors aware of how lifestyle choices can affect the voice. It's mostly a lot of practical things, common sense really: don't drink fizzy drinks before you go on, don't eat hard sharp foods, don't eat dusty foods, hydrate and sleep adequately, and limit alcohol and smoking intake. These are really practical, sensible things but they're easily forgotten in the grand melee of rehearsing!

The actors that I work with often come from different backgrounds and training, and have varying degrees of experience with Shakespeare's text. So, in order for me to work on each voice adequately I have one-to-one sessions structured into the rehearsals. I identify what I need to work on with each performer; it's an opportunity for me to work in parallel with the rehearsal room and give the actors things to put back into the work. Some actors feel it's a tad remedial, and some actors welcome it, especially those who are fresh out of drama school. During these sessions, I help bed sounds into the body. Shakespeare has done the most incredible job already for us; he has laid it out on a plate! It's like a smorgasbord of sounds, a buffet of delicacies. He works with stunning soundscapes, so if we don't chase sense logic or emotional logic, and instead allow ourselves total freedom to investigate these sounds purely as sounds, exploring the vowels and consonants fully, each word becomes its own little architectural sound parcel.

I'm a great believer that you go to the theatre to *listen*, not necessarily to *see* a play. When I go to the theatre I don't really worry about what I see, what I am doing is listening, waiting for the landing of thoughts. The audience may not always be able to see the actor, so the voice has to come through from a very active body. There's the muscularity of thought involved, as well as the physical muscularity of the body promoting that thought, and of course vocal muscularity. An actor needs to produce a sound that is as resonant and as clear as their downstage voice, even when they may be retreating upstage. Nowadays, we have the luxury of previews to check the audibility levels. So, I go around the auditorium and sit in every single seat, including all of the really naff seats, and it's fascinating how, wherever you sit, and wherever the actors are, it creates a different acoustic experience for everybody. It's our job to understand that matrix, which is on three levels – stalls, circle and upper decks at the RST – and make sure everything is clear and effective. It can be tricky for actors who might've done fifteen years' work in a small studio theatre, and suddenly they're in a stadium ... we have to power up the voice and find the stamina required to handle these big spaces.

Once the show is open I will monitor the actors and give feedback regularly. I keep a record of the notes I give so that I can tell by the next performance if they've corrected them or not. Obviously, the performance will always be different, always unique, but if they dip at the end of their phrases, if I don't hear the story, the argument, the rhetoric or if I simply don't hear a word properly, then those problems are essential to address. Once the show is underway directors will leave, movement directors leave, technical designers leave, the creative team leaves – so then it's up to people like me to maintain the integrity of the show. I have to be very careful that I don't direct (of course I'm directing voices) but it's important to recognize I am a part of this mould that the directors have created. I'm trying to encourage the voices to work for the benefit of that vision.

I've used the working methods of the fantastic American director, Anne Bogart, through the years. She has helped me to better understand the relationship between space and text. One of her exercises works on the principle of letting the text inspire you where and how to move. So, if you're very secure with what you're saying, then you move forward; if there's a sense of doubt, you will tend to stay still, or move backwards. Then, you can look at the physical trace forms that the text gives you. Actors will often say, 'The speech took me in a complete circle', or 'I moved in this arc', or 'I felt this sort of tangential quality'. The point of the exercise is to expose the 'map' that is in the text. Shakespeare gives us the geographical pointers in the text. We have the geography as a given – a house interior, a wood, a castle – then there's what I call the 'animate map', or, how the world is peopled. It's not inanimate, far from it! Then once these things are established, that informs the emotional map, how sounds propel us to move or not, because of where we are and who inhabits our scene.

Look at Romeo's speech, 'Tis torture and not mercy: heaven is here' (*Romeo and Juliet*, 3.3.29–51). Throughout that speech he talks about the physical geography, metaphysical states and banishment from Verona and his wife Juliet. This is why (for me) 'blocking' doesn't really work; for me, it's negative, it 'blocks' the actor. Shakespeare has written the map in the text, it just takes a little text-detecting to work it through. In this speech like all his texts, you have got an entire world around you: you're talking about places, people and you can use the text to advise where you are, and how you speak these lines with a visceral and bodily connected nature.

So, when you are responsive to what Shakespeare is giving you, when you trust the sounds, the words, the language, and allow them in, fully and unconditionally, the potential of his genius can be fully realized. It's pure magic!

GREGORY DORAN, ARTISTIC DIRECTOR, RSC

'You go – did he really think all this out?'

The best bit of advice I ever got was from one of my teachers, Rudi Shelly. He used to wag his finger at me and say, 'Greg, don't want to be clever.' I thought that was brilliant, because so often people approach Shakespeare and say, 'I'll do this with it.' When I was doing *Hamlet*, people would say, 'What's your take on *Hamlet*?' as if somehow you have to do something with those plays, more than the play itself. The currency is in danger of being devalued, because of the amount of things we feel we have to do *with* Shakespeare, rather than *do* Shakespeare.

Actors come to Shakespeare wondering, 'How are you going to do this differently?' to prevent the 'if it's Tuesday, it must be *As You Like It*' syndrome, and that is a real danger. It requires a degree of confidence to go 'this play *works*', and the starting point shouldn't be 'how can we make this different?'. Let the starting point be the exploration, because you are different, and the actors' interpretations will be different, because they *are* different.

At university I ran a company of actors from universities and drama schools. What I quickly discovered was that the drama school students, who hadn't been to university, all felt that the university students were too cerebral, that they just wanted to talk about the academics of it; whereas, the university actors, all of whom wanted to be actors eventually, all felt that the drama school students had this thing called technique that they didn't really understand. I think that led me to want to do a postgraduate course at the Bristol Old Vic's school, after I'd done my degree, because what was crucial was seeing the text from both 'sides'. All the brilliant ideas in the world are useless if you couldn't actually be heard or do a line in the iambic pentameter. Similarly, if you could just do the iambic pentameter but there was no substance behind it, then that wouldn't work either.

Verse and text

My approach to text begins really with a series of workshops that I tend now to do. I use the opening two speeches of *Titus Andronicus* (1.1.1–17), or the opening prologue of *Romeo and Juliet* (Prologue 1–14), because the opening prologue has no character associated with it. That doesn't mean that it doesn't have character, and that's what I try and suggest to people. For instance, you can look at the iambic pentameter and get actors to be easy with it by saying, look: it is just basically a heartbeat, a heartbeat that is going through the play. Sometimes the heartbeat jumps, sometimes it sort of goes the other way round, right from the first line. If the play started with the second line, it would go very regularly '*In fair Verona where we lay our scene*' – that is perfectly regular iambic. If you try de-dum de-dumming the first line it goes '*TWO households both alike in dignity*' – so he's grabbing you right in the beginning. Even before he has set up the rhythm, he is breaking it, and he is breaking it with the two words which the whole play is about: two households. There is dysfunction; there is a clash between them. Also, presumably, in the Globe Theatre it was easier to grab people with two words, rather than trying to get their attention with 'In fair Verona'.

Caesurae

Looking at caesurae also becomes really interesting:

> Two households, both alike in dignity –

You've got the caesura – there's the pause – though not really a pause, more of a springboard from one part of the line to the other.

> In fair Verona, where we lay our scene,
> From ancient grudge –

Somewhere round about there is your caesura –

> break to new mutiny,
> Where civil blood made civil hands unclean.

I say, OK, where's the caesura? What about after '*blood*'? Interesting, maybe, or what about before unclean? You can't land it unless you've picked out the rhyme so:

> Two households, both alike in DIGNITY,
> In fair Verona, where we lay our SCENE,

From ancient grudge break to new mutiny,
Where civil blood makes civil hands –

you're waiting for the rhyme, and what is that rhyme –

UNCLEAN.

If you put a caesura in front of '*unclean*', there's your wit: because those hands aren't '*unclean*' – that's the understatement of the year – they're dripping in gore!

Where civil blood, makes civil hands –

what shall we say . . . –

UNCLEAN

. . . and there you've found some evidence of character or wit or personal investment in the thing and then the actor has something to play with.

Rhetoric

I go through a similar process with the two *Titus* speeches. I do it because most people know *Romeo and Juliet*, but very rarely do the actors know intimately *Titus Andronicus*, and the two opening speeches. Saturninus has the first and his brother Bassianus has the second. The exercise is to find out what their characters are like. In eight lines of text I'm trying to teach them not to impose your character or your idea of the character onto it; find out how they speak and you have found your character.

I start the exercise by getting them to work out what it means, to put it into their own words first. Saturninus says something like:

Noble patricians, patrons of my right,
Defend the justice of my cause with arms.

And countrymen, my loving followers,
Plead my successive title with your swords.
I am his first-born son that was the last
That wore the imperial diadem of Rome:
Then let my father's honours live in me,
Nor wrong mine age with this indignity.
(Titus Andronicus, 1.1.1–8)

Whereas Bassianus begins:

Romans, friends, followers, favourers of my right

(9)

You try to find the iambic in the line, and you can't; it's like
John Major taking his jacket off when he was doing that
speech before he became prime minister, and he says, 'I'm just
John, just call me John', and that's what Bassianus is doing.
Then, listen to those 'f's':

Romans, friends, followers, favourers of my right

It's not aggressive, it's not petulant, it's not sort of psychotic in
its rage – it's reasoned; he uses rhetoric.

Then I get somebody to read Saturninus and any time he
mentions me or I or mine, everybody else repeats it. And all
you hear in the room is 'me', 'my', 'I', 'me' and 'mine', and by
the end you get the real sense of his paranoia about his status.

And I then get them both to do it as if it were a party
political broadcast and I get everybody to say who's best. By the
end of it, they conclude that Saturninus is paranoid, malicious,
vindictive and there's a huge list of character traits, and though
you might say that Bassianus is using rhetoric in a skillful and
manipulative way, you might also say that he is just a good guy.

The point of the process is to start off by getting actors to
see how powerful oratory can be: how powerful the tools of
rhetoric are, and then to get them to understand that they need
to look for the clues that are in the text, before they try and
work out who their character is.

I spend a long time with the text. We go round the table, we read the text – nobody is ever to speak their own – and then everybody puts the whole thing into their own words. Hamlet, who is sitting on the one side of the table, who thinks he has worked out what the part is about, will hear Ophelia reading his lines and putting them into her own words. And it makes you attend to the language in a completely different way, and as a group we make a decision about what the play means. It was most potent for me with *King John*. I thought – we are going to work out what this play is, and trust that Shakespeare knows what he is doing, so I'm not going to cut it ... we may cut it, but we will cut it as a process of working out what it means first. By absolutely attending to what each person was saying, and how they were saying it, it became so funny. The company had to be alert to the joy in the language, and that part of the pastime was to let the language be playful. The RSC allowed us the rehearsal time to do this, which permitted those ideas to percolate over time, rather than having to rush those decisions into a production.

I think attending to the world around you is important, and the world around us particularly shifted the meaning and nature of the play one Tuesday afternoon, when at 1.46 (sixteen minutes after a matinee performance had begun) a plane crashed into a tower in New York. Just before the interval the second tower came down, and of course the company were shocked, but the audience knew nothing about it, because the first plane hadn't hit the building by the time the matinee started. In the second act, on TV, 200 people leapt from the buildings, and in the play, the little boy falls from the tower. Jo Stone-Fewings said he didn't know how to go on. He *did* go on, and what we learnt was that Shakespeare gives you the lines: I have learnt to allow the subject of the play to speak to you, and to trust it to do more work than you often allow it to do. Somehow when you get actors and an audience and you trust the language, it'll work.

Actors feel enabled by this knowledge. If they don't like it, they don't have to use it, but if they respond to it, it'll make them more able to own the language. Otherwise you feel, as I did when I joined the company, that Shakespeare is intimidating and that there's some divine panel sitting in, waiting to jump on any errant stress. It is an empowering process to say to actors: this is what you've got there, and I suppose it's what irritates me when you see Shakespeare which pays so little attention to that.

In practice

You don't want it to restrict actors, you want it to release them, and that's the difficulty. I think it's a process of using the knowledge that you have in whichever way is best. I learnt, as a director, very early on in my career that you had to provide the process by which that actor could get to that performance. In *Henry VIII*, for instance, I knew that Ian Hogg playing Wolsey didn't want to talk about what or where that stress needed to fall, until he knew who Wolsey was, and he knew how to play it and he had found his voice. Whereas Jane Lapotaire, playing Katherine, would want to have her speeches blocked. She wanted to marry the rhythm to the muscle memory of the blocking, and you had to provide the structure and environment for both actors to get to their performance. During *Cardenio*, until Lucy Briggs-Owen knew who Lucinda was, there was no point in giving her indications of where the stresses might lie. She would find them, because she would find them through the character.

You have to find a way of engaging people with heightened language, and recognizing that it is heightened language, without trying to make it everyday. I think that the legacy of Peter Hall and John Barton lives in digging the text for the political and for the wit. Cicely Berry's contribution is honouring the violence of the language, and acknowledging the ways the language has a greater richness. I think there's danger if you just chuck that out. Every generation chucks out the previous generation, but, I think there is an awareness now that there is a beauty in the language that you have to find, and it's the most difficult thing to find if your approach is to reduce it to a conversational level.

POLLY FINDLAY, DIRECTOR

There are probably three things I would do, first, when working on a Shakespeare play, and it's probably easiest if I use working on *As You Like It* as the example here.

What's the sentence?

The first thing I would do would be to distill the play into a single sentence: this makes you articulate your own agenda with the play. So, for example, for *As You Like It*, the sentence I came up with was 'a lonely princess obsessed with self-control, learns to let go, and in doing so makes the world a better place' … which actually is the same as the plot of Disney's *Frozen*, isn't it? [*laughter*]. For me, that's what the heart of the play is. Then you make sure that all of your editing decisions are tailored in such a way as to help you tell that particular story; you're using that sentence as a kind of check and balance system to weigh against every editing decision you make. Each edit has to be in service of the pure driving line of that sentence.

What's the post-it note? The second thing I do – and this isn't my idea, it's a version of a Rupert Goold idea – is to find a single adjective to describe the way you want the audience to feel, walking out of the theatre. Once you've found that, you put it on a post-it note and stick it above your desk: for *As You Like It* the word I came up with was 'delighted'; put another way, if the play was to perform a transitive action on the audience, it should be 'to delight them'. So, as the editing decisions had to relate the driving line of the sentence I just mentioned, so the tech and production decisions had to be built around the idea of wanting to delight the audience.

It follows that the sense of delight I wanted at the end of the play would be very dependent on the sense of something else – the opposite – at the beginning: you couldn't possibly put together a production where every *single* gesture was about delighting the audience; that would quickly become meaningless and awful. What you are trying to do is to orchestrate a journey that begins from a point of horror, and moves towards something that is liberating. In this respect, knowing that we had to make the biggest possible journey from A to Z was very helpful for working out (for example) what the Court should be like. I certainly felt that I had seen a lot of productions of the play where the Court felt like a pretty cool place to be: a place you might find in a Sunday supplement, with lots of black and silver surfaces populated by people wearing sunglasses all the time ... in those instances I couldn't quite work out why everybody seemed so desperate to leave it! It felt very important to know what it was they were escaping.

We had to decide what was unique about the *As You Like It* forest compared to the other magical landscapes you find in Shakespeare's plays – the forest in *A Midsummer Night's Dream* or the island in *The Tempest*, for example; the Arden forest is rooted in a very different kind of feeling because there are proper sharecroppers there, and people who are looking after sheep talking about the economics of that, and so on. What we ended up thinking was that the nature of the magic in the forest was precisely the same as the nature of the magic in the theatre, in that, if I say to you in a theatre: 'this iPhone is a baby', as long as the nature of that contract is clear, and the audience is happy to invest in it, we can all totally behave as though this iPhone *was* a baby. At the point which Rosalind says, 'I'm a boy', the quality of the investment in that idea from the world around her is precisely the same as the quality of investment that comes with the theatre. It's about saying, 'I can be anything I want to be' and the 'fact' of that makes it 'true' ... this, we felt, should be the source of the delight. For example, we started in a world governed by one set of theatrical rules, which behaved much more like a conventionally naturalistic play. At the beginning, everything you saw had a kind of grounding reality, it looked like an office with lots of tables and chairs laid out ... and then we exploded these rules: the chairs and tables all pulled up and formed a massive tree sculpture, creating a forest through a change in theatrical vocabulary.

What's the gesture?

The third thing I would do – with any classical play, actually – would be to try to decide: what was the gesture of this play – what was the social function of the play – at the time in which it was written, and how can I best replicate that in a contemporary context? So, for example, when I was doing *Antigone* here at the National, it seems to me that what Sophocles had written for his audience was a kind of political thriller. There seemed to be no point doing anything which was about people dressed in togas; the question was, how do I take this material and make something that feels like a contemporary political thriller out of it, now? And with *As You Like It* I had to answer the same kind of question: if *As You Like It* was written now, what would it be? And at that time I thought it would basically be *The Fast Show* ... I was trying to imagine the experience of the first audiences going to see *As You Like It*, and it did feel something like sketch show. Those scenes, particularly in the second half, don't function like typical Shakespearean scenes ... pretty much nothing happens! If you drew the graph of the plot of *As You Like It* at the point where on the corresponding graph for *Henry V* there would be a *massive* battle, in *As You Like It*, somebody is chatting about how much a sheep costs ... the progression in that play is to do with character development, rather than with plot. I think that what Shakespeare was probably trying to set up was something that felt much more like a series of sketches, that allowed us to see a different facet of the characters each time.

But of course it was impossible for us to take the script of *As You Like It* as it is, and make it feel like it has the energy of a modern sketch show like *The Fast Show*; so what we did was to cut a lot of those scenes into two or three – and because there wasn't any central event, you could get away with doing that – and then splice them, so that the pace of the scene felt three or four times as fast as it might ordinarily have been. And then we borrowed bits of *All's Well That Ends Well* and a couple of other Shakespearean comedies to try and pad it out, and make the whole thing feel faster, funnier and quicker-cut. And to me that feels completely respectful of the original gesture; it's a way of bringing what that gesture was – with its full integrity – to a modern audience. I think this will always unlock something more interesting than trying to honour the author's intention in what might be seen as a more traditional way ... we so often see people trying replicate the performance conditions under which the play was produced, rather than trying to replicate the *sensibility* in which the play was produced.

Units in rehearsal

I think that part of the director's job is to find a bespoke approach to each particular play, because I think different plays exercise different muscles, and it is up to you to identify the particular muscle group required and to build that one up. But having said that, I think that with a Shakespeare play, there are some things that I would probably *always* do. And, the first of those would be a unit-ing exercise.

The cast and I would read through the play collectively, to see if we can find the moments where we can all agree that something changes for the stage; this means, crudely, it has to affect absolutely everybody on stage. And at that point you draw a line across the page and call it a unit. An entrance or an exit is always unit change, a stage direction such as 'it begins snowing' would always be a unit change, and other than that it's something which arrives in the room which 'changes the weather' in the room in some way ... and sometimes it's quite difficult to decide exactly where that is, exactly where the line hits, and the weather changes in a conclusive way.

For example, if one character were to sit down with another and say, 'We need to talk', you could argue that you could draw a line there ... however if that character went on to say, 'There's something I've been meaning to say to you for some time ... I think you should sit down ... I'm pregnant' you would probably have to agree that the unit change should come after 'I'm pregnant', because that line would represent the point where the unit change definitively lands in the room.

What that process produces is an average of two or three units across each page, and these form a sequence of story-building blocks. If you then label each of these in the right-hand margin of the page, finding a one or two word title that summarizes the unit – in this example, the name of the first unit might be 'Big News' – and read down that right-hand column of each page, you end up with a kind of emotional shorthand for the play. This tells you, in a very distilled way, what impact you have to make clear to the audience in each moment of the play. It's a kind of map, showing you what your job is at each moment of the play. Usually it takes about a week to do this exercise, and it feels quite fundamental: if you don't have an exercise like that, it's perfectly possible for any of us to get to the end of the sixth week of rehearsals – particularly of these big complex Renaissance texts – and realize that you never quite knew what was going on, because the tapestry is so densely woven. This is one valuable way of making sure that everyone is literally on the same page.

Paraphrasing in rehearsal

The other thing that I would always do with any Shakespeare play is to get the company to play the play in a very precise paraphrase; sticking to the rhythm of thoughts as much as possible, while putting them into their own words. When we did this exercise with one of the Rosalind–Orlando scenes, it became clear just how much of a reach Ganymede's thoughts are, as a result of the actor being in the position of having to 'busk' their lines in the same way that Ganymede has to. It also made apparent how *weird* some of those thoughts are; if you approach them in a kind of top-down way, playing the poetry rather than the jaggedness of the thoughts underneath, then you end up playing somebody who sort of knows all the answers, in a very arch kind of way, rather than somebody who is fighting desperately for the right thing to say, and doing a just-about-plausible job of that ... and I do think that is sometimes a problem with some of the Rosalinds I've seen. If you can help the actor fight for the thoughts in the same way that the character is always fighting for their thoughts, then something interesting about their personality is always thrown up over the course of that exercise. And of course it also means that everybody knows exactly what they're saying, at any given point. I have often felt that once you've done that exercise enough, once you've really pushed the actor to fight for *precisely* the thought that is on the page, you've done 90 per cent of the work of the scene. I've always found that the most absolutely useful thing.

Influences and inspirations

My work has been informed a great deal by the opportunities I've had to work on such big stages, at such an early point in my career; I owe a debt to the National Theatre in particular. Marianne Elliott is someone I've assisted a lot, and from her I have learnt the most about staging, or how to focus a scene, or how storytelling works in the space. I've also spent quite a lot of time in Germany recently – I redirected *War Horse* in German, in Berlin – and this fed a growing interest in the way they make theatre in mainland Europe. I was able to build up a network of people in Berlin with whom I continue to collaborate. I had found the grand conceptualization of German theatre quite intimidating initially; I felt it must belong to a very different kind of tradition to the one that I felt I had grown up in, which was about fidelity to the text and putting the writer at the centre of the enterprise. But working with these very good artists in Berlin has taught me that their approach to unlocking what the writer's idea might have been may be more radical than mine, but essentially belongs to the same discipline ... and that discovery has been very liberating.

Solving the puzzle

I did *The Alchemist* recently, which was very interesting, having just worked on a Shakespeare play beforehand. I think a Ben Jonson line can look at first glance impossibly complicated: after three days of rehearsal trying to unpick an incredibly carbuncled line, you end up realizing, 'Oh ... he just means, "pimp"!' The experience of working on a Shakespeare line is completely different: the more you look at it, the more possible interpretations open up. The density of Shakespeare's language has all of the appeal of a puzzle, which leads you to think 'I can crack this', but of course you find out that there are so many ways in which that puzzle can be solved, and that you can keep going in your attempts to solve that puzzle over the course of a run. Shakespeare's language just keeps giving, really, doesn't it? That's why people find it such an attractive thing to work with.

LINDSAY KEMP, DANCER

I was born in 1938, near Liverpool; my father's ship was torpedoed at the beginning of the war and his life was lost. My mother and I returned to her family in her hometown of South Shields, where I was soon to begin dancing classes at the age of four. I made my dancing debut entertaining the neighbours, their children and dogs in our communal air-raid shelter, as the bombs were dropping. Our downstairs neighbour Mr Brown sometimes accompanied me on his saxophone. His wife said his playing would attract the enemy planes, and my mother added 'or frighten them off'! I was sad when the war ended and my little audience dispersed.

I was brought up with the English popular theatre, with visits to the traditional pantomime at the Sunderland Empire, where my mother took me every Christmas throughout my childhood. The transformations and ballets were for me the most impressive things about the pantomime. I was intrigued by the cross-dressed principals, and delighted to be part of the audience participation: singing along with the songs, and shouting 'He's behind you!' or 'Oh no you don't!' whenever it was required. The most marvellous part of all was the flying ballet: girls dressed as butterflies flying above the stage, and sometimes through the auditorium. The necessary machinery was usually supplied by Kirby's Flying Ballet: Mr Kirby's grandson flew me several times in later years, first as Puck in *A Midsummer Night's Dream*, and then in *Onnagata*, both productions at Sadler's Wells theatre, and later on, in *Variètè* at the Hackney Empire, one of the famous homes of panto. I made my debut in panto as a chorus boy at Liverpool Empire in the late 1950s. Ken Dodd was the star, and I learned a lot from him about comic timing. A few years later I played Clown in a Victorian-style pantomime at the Edinburgh Lyceum. Ah, those magical transformation scenes achieved with painted gauze and clever lighting! I have often used them in my productions of operas and ballets. I prefer the old ways of creating stage magic.

I danced and entertained throughout my horrible boarding school days; my dances and performances in my little makeshift plays made life bearable. After school I studied dance and drama with the great John Broome at the Northern Theatre School in Bradford, where my mother and I then lived. John had previously studied with Sigurd Leeder, who was a disciple of Rudolf von Laban, and previously associate director with

Kurt Jooss, of the Ballets Jooss. John encouraged me to go to London, where Leeder accepted me as a pupil. John gave me my treasured copy of *My Life* by Isadora Duncan as a farewell gift. He had earlier given me books about Nijinsky, the Ballets Russes and Mary Wigman. While in London I also took classes with Marie Rambert and several other teachers over the years, including Marcel Marceau.

After performing with numerous dance groups, in musicals and cabarets, and in several small Shakespeare productions, I formed my own company to present *Flowers: A Pantomime for Jean Genet* based on Genet's book *Notre Dame des Fleurs*. This was a turning point in my career, and the beginning of my love affair with the avant-garde. Genet led me to Antonin Artaud and the Theatre of Cruelty. I am attracted to all aspects of the theatre, and have enjoyed performing in the streets as much as in opera houses. At school, and in the sometimes-rough working men's clubs where I often performed, I learned the hard way how to put the audience under my spell. In those clubs, the punters had come to see the strippers, and at first were not too happy to see a man in pink tights and white face introduced by the compere as 'The Man Who Mimes His Own Business'.

A Midsummer Night's Dream

Romolo Valli had seen *Flowers* in London and had hoped to take it to the Spoleto Festival, where he was an associate director with Gian-Carlo Menotti. Menotti refused to take the production, as he feared scandal, due to the nudity and homosexuality. He also remembered my dancing partner the Incredible Orlando and me gatecrashing an earlier Festival, where we entertained the crowd dancing and rattling our tambourines in the streets and piazzas for *moneti*. Menotti felt that we had lowered the tone of the Festival, and had us escorted out of town by the Carabinieri. When Romolo Valli became the artistic director of the Teatro Eliseo in Rome he immediately commissioned me to do a production of *A Midsummer Night's Dream*. I was to play Puck, and at last I was able to fly, aided by Kirby's Flying Ballet!

I didn't take into account how painful and terrifying flying would be. It was odd that I insisted on flying, as I suffer from extreme vertigo, but it was all for the audience's pleasure. Acting involves taking risks, playing dangerously ... this brings the essential element of excitement to the theatre. Risk is an essential part of performance, even though it can have disastrous results, sometimes! My tradition, my roots tell me that you've got to thrill an audience, walking the tightrope where they sense you could fall ... as I occasionally did.

I enjoy using my voice, and I have used it in a number of my own productions, including *Salome, Woyzeck, The Maids*, in several Shakespeare productions, and films, including Ken Russell's *Savage Messiah* and Robin Hardy's *The Wicker Man*. I suffer the fear of forgetting my words, which only makes my constant stage fright worse, which in the end is my fear of disappointing the audience.

Making *A Midsummer Night's Dream*

'Tonight Is So Right for Love', a song by Elvis Presley where he sings about 'a midsummer night's dream', was my first inspiration and starting point for the show. I collected relevant images, and designed costumes inspired by the Victorian fairy paintings by Henry Fuseli and others, including Richard Dadd and William Blake. I made the sketches while listening to Mendelsohn's incidental music to the play. I was also greatly inspired by Max Reinhardt's film, especially by Nijinska's choreography and the performance of Mickey Rooney as Puck.

I worked closely with my friend the Spanish composer Carlos Miranda on the score, which also included ethnic (African and Indian) and Spanish music. The company sang the Mendelsohn songs from the play. Carlos played one of the Mechanicals, and accompanied himself on his piano-accordion when not in the pit playing his harpsichord while conducting the small orchestra. Some recorded dialogue was woven into the musical tapestry. After playing the Elvis song, and before the curtain rose, I made my entrance as Puck, emerging through a trap-door, accompanied by the strains of Offenbach's *Barcarolle*, and the voice of John Gielgud reciting part of 'My gentle puck, come hither' (*A Midsummer Night's Dream*, 2.1.148–74). This was mixed with the voice of Mickey Rooney, and the sound of exotic birds.

For the text, I used the speeches of Oberon and Titania, which I loved, and had committed to memory as a child, rather than going to a full script and deciding what to cut. One of the reasons I didn't incorporate more dialogue into my *Dream* was because we toured the show extensively through Italy, Spain and South America, before going on to perform in Japan, and other parts of the world. I didn't want to distance the audience by performing in a language which they did not understand. I directed the production as I would an opera. The rhythms and the musicality of Shakespeare's language can make the meaning clear for any audience, provided the actor has sufficient training, technique and talent. There isn't time in rehearsals to teach these skills if they are not already there. These days the actor is rarely equipped with all the performer's skills which were once *de rigueur*. In the past, the acrobatic harlequin in pantomime at Drury Lane was often seen, some nights later, playing Shakespeare; in later years, Robert Helpmann successfully played Hamlet at Stratford upon Avon, and afterwards, danced the same role in his ballet at Covent Garden. Today, the actor's training often lacks breadth and body: dance is often not included in drama school courses, and if it is, there's not enough of it.

My experience of working with dancers and actors is that very few of them have much grounding in the history of their art form, and few explore the related arts – painting, music, literature and the cinema. It's sad to see that so few young actors and dancers are interested in what went before: if you don't explore what went before, and learn from that, the present lacks depth and perspective. We see so much today that is superficial, without roots in the heart, or passion. Shakespeare knew what had gone before, and how little human nature changes over the centuries: he didn't invent his plots, but he reinvented and reimagined many tales that had proved themselves effective in the past.

Romeo and Juliet

I remembered *Romeo and Juliet*, through the famous speeches, and the movements, especially the gestures of the lovers' hands. The production I did with students in Verona was a dance-drama, with music as varied as live percussion, Spanish and Italian Renaissance music, George Crumb, Handel and Purcell's *Dido and Aeneas*. I was attracted to Shakespeare's themes of light, meaning freedom. This allowed me to incorporate the motif of a bird in flight. At the end of the piece, the lovers transfigure and ascend to the heavens, to *Lascia ch'io pianga* (from Handel's *Rinaldo*) carrying the audience with them. Rebirth is a constant theme in all my work, and so my version of the play ends with this hope ... lifting the spirits of the public.

ETHAN McSWEENY, DIRECTOR

Language

The beauty of Shakespeare's language is that it is so informative and so rich that it allows you to mine every line for multiple layers of meaning. Clues in the text reveal themselves most fully when you are able to experience the language as a living, breathing thing; that's why so often what we get to do in rehearsal, repeating and hearing it over and over again, exceeds the experience of the average member of the public who only perceives it on the page. It's not the same thing even to just have it read aloud and frankly, I don't know for sure that we do Shakespeare a very good service by reading him aloud in high school English classes (although I do get why that is important), because so few of us can read it at that stage. For the performer, the language requires a dexterity of thought and emotion and muscle that takes years to develop. I was very fortunate because when I graduated from university, I went straight to be the assistant director at the Shakespeare Theatre in Washington DC, where I worked on probably twenty to twenty-five Shakespeare plays over four years. I discovered that Shakespeare *is* a language, and that you learn a kind of fluency by listening to people who know how to speak it, speaking it all the time. Over time, your own ear develops a kind of natural sense of what the cadence of a line is, which for the most part fits quite naturally into our own patterns of speech, and you become accustomed to the occasional idiosyncrasies of syntax that are present in any language.

So much of Shakespeare is about rhythm. I believe there is a distinct 'music' in his texts. It's one of those things that sets him apart from his contemporaries and why you can usually tell when a play is not by Shakespeare, when it's by Marlowe, or by Jonson, because the rhythm of the words doesn't have quite the same suppleness. There is a kind of ease in Shakespeare's writing that just flows. More often than not, if the rhythm of the line is correct, the sense comes through.

Rhythm is especially crucial when we're looking at comedy, which can be some of the hardest and most rewarding material Shakespeare wrote, because trying to figure out how to make it live for a contemporary audience can be extremely challenging. More often than not, part of the joke is built into the rhythm of the telling. It isn't so much that rhythm *equals* meaning, but if you get the rhythm right the laugh will land, and it isn't entirely dependent on full comprehension of every last word by the listener, it's about ba-dum ba-dum ba-dum ba-dum da-DUM. It is important to avoid 'explication' as there is nothing either dramatic or funny about an actor explaining or demonstrating what a line means. What is important is the action that underlies the line.

But you have to work very hard to carefully build the comedy logic of a bit of business from one moment to the next while making sure that what is described in the text remains true. When I was working under Garland Wright on his last production of *The Tempest*, we were in tech doing Caliban, Trinculo and Stephano's first scene with the 'beast' with four legs, and two voices and three heads (*The Tempest*, 2.2) … and it took us about four hours to work out how to do it with the gabardine … I remember Garland's voice on the 'god mic' saying – 'It's comforting to know that since Burbage and Kemp for four hundred years, actors have been struggling with this same bit of business.'

Moment to moment

The first thing I do with a performance script, and I learned this on Shakespeare but I do it with any text I am going to direct, is to create a detailed scene breakdown into 'French scenes' (loosely based on characters' entrances and exits). Doing so helps me perceive the structure of the play separate from what assumptions we might have about it.

Breaking the script down is also my way of slowing myself and all of us down, getting us not looking at the big picture, but at the small pieces. And then, as we go into rehearsal we start to look at ever-smaller units, so maybe, scene by scene, line by line. If we have someone who has time, and that may not be a director, that may be a voice and speech coach, we may look at it word by word, syllable by syllable – you know, until you get to the smallest unit. I work 'moment to moment', which means, asking what is happening in this moment and then what has to happen to get to the next moment? Another way of describing 'moment to moment' is really 'thought to thought' and the challenge is to think each thought and not move so quickly from one to the next that you trip and fall. When you treat it very simply, Shakespeare responds exceptionally well to this kind of 'moment to moment' approach, and it quite readily makes sense.

The other day, I thought about a Liviu Ciulei quotation: 'We have a lot to do, and very little time, so we must work slowly.' I often find myself reflecting on that at the beginning of rehearsals. It occurs to me now that the moment-to-moment approach is about slowing us down, and one of my biggest jobs as a director is just to ask, 'What did you just say? What does that mean? If that is what that means, then why and how does that influence what you say *next?*'

We usually spend about a week around the table really interrogating the text. I like to spend so long around the table that everyone is *dying* to get up on their feet, but also it is important to build the scaffolding of meaning, because if you don't know what you're saying, how in the world are you going to know what to do while you're saying it? It's not even about 'what do I want?'; you can try on different motivations and intentions, and you can keep trying different ones right through performances if you like. But it is about understanding the thoughts and comprehending the meaning and finding its expression in a playable action. In fact, that's what Shakespeare tells us to do. He tells us *exactly* how to do his plays in *Hamlet*; the advice to the players is to speak clearly, to think directly, to act moment by moment and to '[s]uit the action to the word, the word to the action' (3.2.17–18). One of the most important cautions he adds is, don't do too much: don't saw the air, don't tear a passion to tatters, don't gild the lily, don't out-Herod Herod, 'o'erstep not the modesty of nature' (3.2.19). My approach is learn from the language; let it teach you, rather than decide what you're going to *make* it do.

Ultimately, although I'm interested in what it means, what I'm really interested in is what it *does* and what is happening. What is the action? How does it play? What does it do to the other character that makes them do something to you? That's the level of comprehension I try to achieve with the words.

Directorial concepts

Directors all have a point of view, but I think it goes wrong when you try and work externally to come up with a concept, rather than trusting that your 'internal concept' will be different from anyone else's, by virtue of the fact that there are different things in the text that you're going to respond to, and different themes you're going to amplify. I don't know that a conductor approaching a symphony has a concept, and yet every one of them is going to bring a different experience to the narrative arc of that piece of music. So, I think the reason concept gets a bad name is that there are some directors who do things *to* plays, and that's not very nice. However, there is a big difference between doing something *to* a play and doing something *with* a play and I think we are obligated to the latter ... but there is a wide range of options available, of course.

In his book *On Directing Shakespeare* (1989) Ralph Berry identifies four pertinent categories of setting that I have found an excellent distillation of the infinite possibilities:

1. Elizabethan: You can do it in the period in which the play was first performed.

2. Period Envelope: You can do it either in the period in which the play is set (so Roman plays in whatever your idea of ancient Rome is) or in a different analogous period that you find evocative or relevant – I set a *Merchant of Venice* on the Lower East Side of New York in the 1920s, for example, because I wanted the different ethnic groups to be competing with one another for access to a higher class 'Belmont', and I placed a *Much Ado* in revolutionary Cuba in order to take advantage of both the political and cultural background (and partly because everyone else was setting *Much Ado* in nineteenth-century Italy!).

3. Contemporary: This means whatever our 'now' is.

4. The Future: That can be distant or quite near. In
   the 1980s I recall we were all interested in a 'post-
   apocalyptic nuclear winter' so our vision of the future
   is a constantly changing thing. I'd say right now many
   'futuristic' settings tend to imagine a corporation
   dominated post-climate change apocalypse. (I guess
   'apocalypse' seems to be a theme – happy and benign
   futures probably don't make for good drama.)

All those options are all on the table, but also different
venues and different companies call for different directorial
responses. Sometimes I'm conscious of the production history
of a certain play within a certain community, or within the
national discourse. Though I think the quest to be different
can too easily lead one down some false paths, one can try at
least to expose an audience to alternative possibilities within a
'familiar' play: I am about to embark on a *Twelfth Night*, for
example, and I am realizing it is important to me to create a
world 'before' Viola arrives in Illyria, because in my estimation
'Illyria' was as much a state of mind as an actual place, especially
when one considers Shakespeare's own limited travel and thus
circumscribed sense of geography. I think sometimes season
planning considerations and the time of the year can be also
influential; when I was doing a production of *The Tempest*
that was going to be playing over the holiday season at the
Shakespeare Theatre, knowing something about the character
of the audience there, I knew my production needed to appeal
to as wide an audience as possible because there were going to
be people of all ages present.

Shakespeare's 'universality'

Over the course of his career, Shakespeare wrote for a
very broad audience, from absolutely illiterate peasants
to exceptionally well-read, multilingual nobility. He was
eminently capable of communicating effectively across that

wide a spectrum, with jokes that play to the groundlings, and jokes that went way over their heads (and some jokes that are beneath everyone that I think he just could not resist). It is that mix that makes Shakespeare so great. I have a theory about the mix, which is: children love Shakespeare, because children are used to looking at grown-up behaviour and synthesizing narrative out of that behaviour. They don't get bothered by not understanding every last word, because actually they don't understand every last word in their day-to-day lives! Grown-ups, on the other hand, occasionally find themselves quite frustrated if they feel like they're missing something. So, I think it's my job to make sure grown-ups don't feel like they're missing anything, and I think it's easy for people to underestimate how much work goes into making a moment or thought so inevitable that an adult will never for a second think, 'I didn't get it.' I strive for clarity of intention with the actors to produce clarity of meaning for the audience, while endeavouring never to descend to explanation.

We took my 2014 production of *A Midsummer Night's Dream* to China to open the Macao Arts Festival, and it was absolutely incredible how the Chinese audience went for Bottom and the play within the play, to a degree I have never seen elsewhere. They were applauding every laugh – I mean they would laugh, and *then* they would cheer – and to me this was absolute proof that Shakespeare is universal. We give a lot of lip service to that idea, but it turns out to be really true because Shakespeare understands so much about our common humanity. Nevertheless, if you happen to have English as your first language, you're very lucky, because you get to read this stuff in the original. And that is such an incredible privilege.

I often find myself reminding actors that people have not changed in 400 years *at all* – we are exactly the same. We love the same, we fear the same, we fight the same, we die the same. I think that the single biggest difference between Shakespeare's time and ours is probably that we have different bathing customs now and a slightly higher hygiene level! No … (I was kidding) … the real biggest difference now is how our communications platforms have evolved, and that is something that even in his genius Shakespeare could not foresee. While I do enjoy doing discovering 'contemporary' settings with a Shakespeare play, I generally feel that cell phones get in the way. For instance, if the Friar has a cell phone then Romeo doesn't have to die; it would be too easy to fix that problem, with one text message.

A man of the theatre

When I look at the plays, I see very clearly a working person of the theatre just like me (only much, much smarter), struggling to make a living, struggling to produce, capitalizing on a hit and putting something that works in one play into another one, because it *worked* the last time. That means I often find that the simplest, most practical answer to a text question to be the most compelling and I think those can easily get lost in the sheer volume of academic consideration around all aspects of Shakespeare's life, work and literature. That said, I wouldn't want to trivialize the great value in understanding the political, cultural and historical context around the creation of these plays – so I guess I remain a bit of a post-modernist after all. I just think he was probably working to a deadline, in some years churning out nearly three plays a year (long hand!), which is a ridiculous volume to be demanding of yourself if you're also performing, producing and managing a company. These days, a career output of fifteen, maybe twenty plays would be considered *major*. Shakespeare wrote more than thirty-five, give or take.

I do remain quite curious about the given circumstances of his play production, and in the chronology of the plays, and what that might tell us about how he was writing. For example, the fact Lady Macbeth and Cleopatra come so close together must have meant there was a boy actor in the company who was clearly more gifted than all the others, so that Shakespeare could suddenly write those incredibly dynamic and powerful women's roles. And there are clearly other years where writing to the strengths of his actors produced different results.

A quick anecdote about this kind of theatre archaeology that the practitioner can sometimes stumble into: at the Shakespeare Theatre in the 1990s we did *Henry IV, Part 1 and 2* in a single evening, and the next year we followed that with *Henry V*, and the actor that played Falstaff played the captain Gower. There's a moment late in *Henry V* after Agincourt where Fluellen and Gower are talking, and Fluellen asks the name of 'the fat knight' (4.7.47) and Gower says one line – 'Sir John Falstaff' (50) – and that's it. There's no reason for it. No rhyme nor scansion served. So, we were doing it, and the actor who'd played Falstaff the season before just instinctually turned front and said, 'Sir John Falstaff', and the audience spontaneously applauded … and it made complete sense! Shakespeare wrote in a little curtain call: a call back bow that maybe also advertised a revival: come back next week, we're going to be presenting *Henry IV*! I love those things. To me, there's a strong, beating heart of a really practical person confronting eminently practical problems, and it's deeply comforting, as Garland said, to know that theatre people have been struggling the same way throughout recorded time, and that Shakespeare was probably no different. He was a human being, and that's why you ultimately learn most about Shakespeare by looking within yourself. You are your own sounding board for this, and at different times, different bits of the plays might speak to you in different ways depending on where you are in your life and what your experiences are.

BRUCE O'NEIL, HEAD OF MUSIC, RSC

Music in Shakespeare

Shakespeare plays are stuffed with music; they're very musical pieces. Whether that's a character referencing music, someone brought on to sing a song for the other characters, or the music being a full company experience. The songs don't often move the plot along hugely but they do serve a dramatic purpose for Shakespeare. The majority of the references to music in the stage directions are military sounds – heralding the arrival of someone important like a king or queen. That particular music would have been instantly recognized in Shakespeare's day; there was a particular language and syntax to military music, so people would have recognized a specific phrase meaning a specific thing. If Shakespeare says a 'tucket' is sounded, people would have known what that sound meant; it had an influence on what was going on and it became a dramatic function.

One of the major differences between Shakespeare's day and modern-day practice is that the characters on stage would have heard the music that was happening and been aware of it. Whereas now, we're used to cinematic underscoring and music happening without the characters being aware, but it's reinforcing the audience's reaction to what's going on – that was not the case in Shakespeare's day. When I work on a Shakespeare nowadays, there is always the conversation about both the central, diegetic music that Shakespeare has given us, and then any other music that might be added by the overall directorial concept.

Sometimes those things may clash in certain productions, depending on the setting, period and the vision for the piece. The entrance of an army, for example, is always a specific sound depending on where you are in time and place – so you might have to achieve that in a slightly different way to how Shakespeare first intended. You modify the form but the function is still exactly the same.

I remember Marianne Elliott's 2006 production of *Much Ado About Nothing* that was set in Cuba. As soon I heard it would be set there I immediately knew we had been given a gift, musically. Even if you don't know Cuban music, the country has such an identity musically, such a distinctive quality, that you immediately believe it has stylistic integrity and a sound. So, when a production like that is set in a particular locale and perhaps a particular period – it's a gift for a composer. When you are without a period or setting to guide you, the music takes on more of an abstract quality. David Farr's 2012 production of *The Tempest* had a set which was a huge glass box that was Prospero's cell. The music was influenced by the set and the materials that made up the world of the play; a lot of the sounds from the band were from instruments like a bowed vibraphone, harmonics on strings, delicate and brittle sounds. When the spirits and Ariel sang, they used high-pitched tones to reinforce the idea that we're on the more abstract side of things. What's in the text still happens in the way that Shakespeare would have expected; it's just that what we hear is new and different.

Rupert Goold's 2011 production of *The Merchant of Venice* was set in Las Vegas. There's an example of where music is required in obvious places – like the casket opening scenes – and it worked incredibly well because the music was done like the theme for the TV game show *Who Wants to Be a Millionaire?* when you have a bed of intense music underscoring the casket-choosing scene. Goold also introduced snatches of ultra-contemporary recorded music, where characters were listening to it on headphones or in an elevator, peppering his contemporary world with contemporary music doesn't appear in the text at all. It's an inductive approach, which exposes the audience to the same experiences that the characters are having. The cinematic device of having music as underscore that the characters on stage don't hear influences our emotional response to what they're doing. Again, that ties in with the inductive quality that music absolutely has; it has a language and a meaning of its own, which we recognize and respond to.

Music and the 'lizard brain'

Daniel Levitkin wrote a book title *This Is Your Brain on Music* (2007) about the evolutionary basis from which we react to music. There's a part of our brain called the 'lizard brain' which is an earlier evolved part; that area reacts to music in a way that has nothing to do with cultural reference, but is purely about survival. Hearing very loud sounds creates a startle effect, whereas very low tones can make us feel slightly concerned or scared ... as perhaps the rumble of a herd of elephants coming towards us from a distance might do. When we get goosebumps or shivers listening to music it's actually more to do with the 'lizard brain' side of things. When I hear the final movement of Beethoven's Ninth Symphony, that's my goosebump moment: though it could be said to be partly a cultural thing, I think there's also some 'lizard brain' going on, too.

Recognizing what music can do to an audience from a purely visceral point of view is very useful for a director. If you watch a film or a play and the music is having an effect on you, the cultural reference is telling you something, and the evolutionary power of music is the other half of the equation. But there's something else going on underneath as well. That's why the music from any setting or period is powerfully suggestive to the audience in the desired way. Music is so ubiquitous now, and it is so easy these days to obtain just about any piece of music, that in some ways we've become less persuaded of that little bit of magic going on. When you listen to a recording of a very big complex orchestral piece it's not the same as hearing it in the room. You hear things in the room that you don't hear on the recording because when the air is being moved at a live concert, it's reaching your ears, and your brain is doing this unbelievable job of interpreting what is going on; you just don't get that from a recording.

The harmonic series and music psychology

In Shakespeare's day, they were used to hearing a lot of music, not only in theatre but beyond that, and music was part of a wider understanding of the world they were living in. There was an intellectual debate raging at the time about the 'music of the spheres' which refers back to Pythagoras passing the blacksmith's shop and hearing different notes on the anvil; different notes depending on the weight of the hammer on the anvil and the quality of the metal. This sparked the theory of harmonics: if you've got a length of string and you pluck it to get a note, if you halve that length of string and pluck again, you get an octave above. It sets out the series of harmonics which leads to our musical scale, effectively. The psychology behind music is a universal thing.

A pentatonic scale is built by stacking up perfect fifths. Going back to the harmonic series, let's imagine you've cut your piece of string in half to get the octave above. If you halve that string again, the second harmonic is the perfect fifth; the first harmonic is an octave so it's one note and then the same note an octave up. If you then halve that string again, the second harmonic is a perfect fifth. A popular video on YouTube shows Bobby McFerrin demonstrating how an audience can predict the sequence of notes in the pentatonic scale, and this absolutely indicates that it's a universal thing. So if you play a C, then a G, then a D, then an A and an E, the human brain responds to it, and understands it without any learned musical knowledge, because it's part of the harmonic series.

When Hermione's statue wakes up in *The Winter's Tale*, he [Shakespeare] turns to music to express this magical quality, which is absolutely to do with the harmonic series: if you have a piano and you press down the keys so that the damper isn't on the string, and you press another key an octave below, that open string will vibrate in a sympathetic resonance. As it says in Shakespeare's Sonnet 8:

> Mark how one string, sweet husband to another,
> Strikes each in each by mutual ordering,
> Resembling sire, and child, and happy mother,
> Who all in one, one pleasing note do sing:

Whose speechless song being many, seeming one,
Sings this to thee: 'Thou single will prove none.'

                                                    (9–14)

One string starting to vibrate if you plucked another becomes
a metaphor for so many other things, the biggest one being the
Universe itself. So, that's partly why music is absolutely stuffed
in these plays, because it was a fascination of Shakespeare's,
and it could be seen as a kind of magic.

TOM PIPER, DESIGNER

My first point of contact with a new project varies on the style
of the piece and what that piece requires. Of course, there is
the text, that is a given, but I don't tend to get bogged down
in scholastic stuff about which Folio to use. There's also the
second thing I suppose all practical interpreters of Shakespeare
have, which is the back catalogue that one is kind of aware of,
the sort of prior knowledge of seminal productions that one
cannot escape consciousness of.

So, in the process, you will begin of course by reading the
plays, trying to read them in a way so as to fool yourself that this
is the first time you've read this play, and so don't know what's
going to happen. One works alone for a while, maybe writing
down themes, sometimes some people storyboard scenes. I don't
tend to do that because I find it kills your enjoyment of the play if
you have to work out every single moment that happens. I tend to
do little sketches of moments that might inspire me. Quite often
these are completely impractical, and then what you discover
as you work through the process is that these impractical ideas
plant a seed that might bear practical fruit later on.

It always cracks me up when I sit behind some people in the
audience and they look at the set and say, 'Well they haven't

spent very much on the set' before the show even begins. There is an expectation somehow that the designer is creating this sort of giant painting that will then be inhabited by actors, that looks great even without people on it. In fact, the design is actually a sort of sculptural medium that happens over time. The design fulfils its purpose based on the way the actors change it. The costumes, the stories, the use of light: these are the things that occupy the design over time and make it work theatrically.

Developing design ideas

I try not to create a prescriptive solution for every moment, or for every question the text raises. You have to trust that if it worked in the Globe, then it will work here. You've got the possibility of things coming from below, the possibility of things coming from above, you've got your heaven, your hell, your earth. You've got some doors at the back, and a possibility of some reveal. That's all that Shakespeare had, and that's what he wrote his plays for, so if you've got those kinds of elements in there, then you can explore.

No matter how meticulously you try and plan a design, you have to allow for ideas that will develop out of rehearsals. In a production of *A Midsummer Night's Dream* I worked on, the actor playing Starveling started experimenting with the idea of blowing bubbles, or having a blow-up balloon to be the moon. That brought in a little idea that nudged its way through the piece as a kind of layer. It began as something small: when Bottom first appears as an ass Starveling is holding a balloon and then he lets it go in shock and it kind of farts its way around the room; then later on, when the mechanicals meet and they've lost Bottom, one of them is standing there holding this little balloon, and someone punctures it. So you think OK, we've gone far enough down the balloon gag route; then, when he turns up as Moonshine in the mechanicals play, he's got a balloon again, with a light bulb inside it this time, as if to say,

'Yeah the moon is a balloon, now I'm done.' But we don't stop there. For the final dance, Starveling appeared on the back wall and started waving his balloon around. Then more and more balloons flew down to join him so that suddenly he was creating the stars and they were all kind of coming down as balloons with light bulbs. At the end, there was Puck doing his final oratory to these little balloon stars that are around; and that was a design idea that just completely developed through rehearsals.

Providing context

I remember that the first twenty minutes of that production were quite tricky for an audience because they didn't quite know where they were, because we didn't give them very many clues. It meant they had to focus on what the people were saying to find out where we were. The audience had to engage their imaginations to create the world of the play so then gradually stage pictures started happening. There's an easier approach that gives you a lot of information up front, so that a person in the audience thinks, 'OK, I know where I am. It's going to be kind of like this', and that approach has its benefits too sometimes, though the spontaneity and mystery of the idea burns out a lot quicker, as the audience are far more passive in the engagement with the play.

I also think with Shakespeare the big decision is the whole issue of period, that is, where we are going to set it, and when. No matter how you try to avoid it, basically every act of putting a Shakespeare play on stage is an interpretation, even if you decide that the actors are just going to stand there in their ordinary clothes.

I would normally look either at Shakespeare's own period or at the period that we are in now, or at the period that he was writing the play for. It always seems to me if you then introduce another layer – 'let's do it in Nazi Germany' – you're forcing real history to line up with a Renaissance story. So you are looking from our modern point of view, back to 1930s and 1940s Germany, and back to the sixteenth or seventeenth century. Actually, it's impossible to be historically accurate; there are too many layers. If you look at photographs of different versions of Elizabeth I from different ages – from Greta Garbo, through to Glenda Jackson through to Cate Blanchett – you find they all look, with retrospect, like their own period. It's the 1960s version of Elizabeth or it's the 1930s version, as seen in the make-up, the choice of fabrics, the colours they wear: you can't get away from your own time, it's always there. So it's a choice about how many of those kinds of layers you put in there, and certainly with some productions I've worked on we have made a very conscious decision to play with those layers.

In *As You Like It*, we began the play in a very cold, hard but beautiful sort of Elizabethan Protestantism; all the clothes were constricting, and black and white. Then gradually, both through the medium of changing the seasons, and by removing layers and changing things subtly, we moved from there into a world which was virtually modern. That's the only time I think I've managed to make that really work without it jolting. For example, Orlando ended the first half still wearing his leather jerkin but he changed into some modern trousers underneath; the colours were all kind of sympathetic to what he had been wearing before. In the second half he had a leather jacket, the same colour as the jerkin. It was a modern one so his look changed subtly and that's what attracts me, the kind of journey of period that you can do. The audience begin thinking they are watching a period production and slowly got sucked into a world that was very nearly their own.

As a designer, you are thinking about how you can control and influence what people see at given points in the story. In a proscenium arch theatre, all focus goes towards the stage, a shared focus point over which you have a large element of control. However, in a thrust space you know that people will be looking across it, at fellow members of the audience. That instantly means you can't be as controlling about what people are looking at, because there will always be mess, uncontrollable mess, sometimes very funny mess. When we did the Histories the first time in the Swan, there was a woman who had, for some strange reason, brought with her a two-foot-high toy of Kermit the Frog to watch the play with. She was in the second row. That required a lot of concentration on the text by both actors and other audience members. These challenges of the thrust stage mean you have to think as a sculptor: the design will be seen by people from lots of different angles, and therefore the imagery that you create has to work in that variety of sightlines and viewpoints. It has to also work *with* that background of people that you don't necessarily want to be there when you think about it in isolation.

I enjoy the thrust stage because of that communal relationship where actors and audience share the same air in the same room: you can bleed the actors into the space and it doesn't feel as fake as if you are trying to do that under a proscenium house. The actors and the director can recruit the audience to be the lords, to be the soldiers or whatever they need, exactly as Shakespeare's actors would have used the groundlings. When we did *Henry IV, the Comedy of Falstaff*, in that moment when he is recruiting this band of crappy soldiers, he actually picked on one little chunk of the audience to work with. He made them all stand up as potential recruits before saying, 'Oh god, you're rubbish'; the audience involved thought it was funny and everyone else thought it was brilliant that these people were being picked on, rather than them. On the thrust stage you've got that kind of communal relationship going on. So while that's less a design thing, I suppose the design is in the community of the space that is one room and therefore, we can share it.

I know that some designers don't like the thrust because it removes that element of control. There are some schools of designers who design because they have a very strong image in their head. For each character, they'll do a drawing and *that* will be the character for them. What they will really want to do from that point is to make the actors look like that image they have in their head. Because I know there is one of me and twenty-five actors all thinking about their character, I try and let their choices alter my design, and then my design can help specify their choices. You are trying to allow individuality, allowing the needs of that actor to come through. That feels to me a better response.

Another thing that Michael [Boyd] does very well is that he uses the 'rule of three' to test if an idea has earned its place on stage. It can't just be there to be used once, it has to be used several times, and each time it's used the meaning multiplies. With the Histories that meaning just went on and on and on, the resonance of it: it got more sophisticated than the rule of three, but over the whole sequence of plays there was a sort of family of images that repeated, that people in the audience will pick up on and connect with the last time they saw that image. Each time they see it, it has more weight, and they contemplate it more.

I tried to costume people in the histories so that each new character and actor was informed by their previous character and themselves as an actor. You became aware of them as actors as well as their characters, so there was never any attempt to give them false beards or different noses or wigs. I think we only had about two wigs in the whole show, so the audience got the story of how that actor changed and developed as they went through the cycle of plays.

Some designers and directors strive towards a sort of naturalism, but giving people a naturalistic image of a world to begin with sometimes doesn't sit very true with the non-naturalism of Shakespeare's writing. There is a danger that you can fall between two stools. The first big show we did here (RST) was *Much Ado About Nothing* and I think, in retrospect, we kind of fell between two stools. We tried to be quite abstract with some of the ideas and quite comically surreal. For example, when Benedick was hiding, he hid in a tree; there was a tree growing in the middle of a kind of courtyard space, which looked quite naturalistic, although it was bursting through the floorboards, and there was a ceiling.

Benedick hid up in this tree, and then he fell out of the tree when he heard the first news that Beatrice loves him. Then he hid under a table and moved around under the table, a bit like Dougal from *The Magic Roundabout*, which I found very funny. But lots of people found that this idea wasn't within the naturalistic style of what they thought they were looking at. It was too surreal, because surely Benedick would know that by moving, he was no longer hidden? For us, he was behaving with a child's logic which is 'because you can't see me, you can't see what I'm doing', so he was hiding in a really crap way, which for me made it all the funnier. And then at the end he got out of the table by going 'God', you know, 'Beatrice loves me'. Then he went off in one direction. Then we had a crew member come out of a little trap, unseen, and go under the table and the table went off in a different direction. For me, this was a really lovely, old-style comedy device, but we got some of the worst reviews we've ever had for that show, because people thought we were forcing those ideas on the play. I think, in retrospect, if we'd had a more abstract space – if it had been a pure white box with a tree in it – then that kind of idea probably would have worked much better. The problem was, we had set up a semi-naturalistic, Italian courtyard, so people were slightly confused by the more surrealistic twists we were making.

Another policy I have inherited from Michael [Boyd] is an avoidance of scene changes. I now find it incredibly difficult to watch any Shakespearean production where there are scene changes. I think, 'We don't need this, Shakespeare didn't have scene changes.' In the plays one idea impacts on the next idea, so you will have one scene following hard on the end of heels of the previous scene. This means that the characters in the second scene are almost aware of the 'ghost' of the previous scene. The audience watch somebody disappear and then that charges the following scene. Scene changes disrupt that.

Each designer develops from a certain tradition of design. I worked as an assistant in Peter Brook's company on *La Tempête* in 1990. I saw the *Mahabharata*, and I think that kind of shook my perceptions of what theatre design should be. You think it's going to be some big technological epic and actually it wasn't. It was about going into this space, the atmosphere in it, with just the light, the temperature and the simple idea of red earth on the walls; it was about a communal relationship to that space, and it was very much an actor-driven thing. Going to work on *The Tempest* as an assistant designer was a learning curve. I was just making props and set models, but seeing the way that an actor might inform design was fascinating. Chloe Obolensky [the lead designer] said, 'I think there might be a little boat, we might try and use that in the storm', because in *The Tempest*, going from the storm to the island is always the most difficult thing to accomplish. We had a little orange box that we hung on a string, and we had lots of silly ideas, and then I said I would make something: I made a little rough boat out of some wood in the basement. Bouffes du Nord is a bit like a fringe theatre, with only three members of staff and no workshop, so I made this little boat and then gave it into the rehearsals and the actor playing Ariel put it on his head. Then we added some little red sails to it, and it became this sort of hat. Then he came on running with it and he described the storm using this little boat, and that became one of the images of the production. No one ever did a sketch of it, nobody ever drew it all up, it just happened; we gave the raw material to the actor, and let them play with it, to see what would come from that rehearsal.

But at Bouffes du Nord you were always running behind the imagination of the actors. Someone would say, 'We need some puppets', so you'd spend about three days improvising some puppets. By the time you got to rehearsal with any puppets they'd moved onto something else. In the end of course he [Brook] would inevitably do something completely different, much simpler and much more beautiful. You could see him, even with his great experience, going from a very complicated idea, trying to distil it and trying to come up with the essence of how to create an image that is witty, that is moving and that actually is fulfilled by the actors. I suppose I see myself as belonging to that tradition of design. It doesn't stop me designing big sets sometimes, or creating big structures, or having ideas that things might whizz up or around or whatever; but I try wherever possible to remember that there is going to be an actor at the heart of it.

RENATO ROCHA, DIRECTOR

Approach to Shakespeare

The first step is always identifying how this story is still relevant nowadays – what it does to us now, and what its relationship to contemporary society is. I did a lot of work with the great, famous Shakespeare plays at the beginning of my career, but after my experiences with educational and social projects in favelas and the peripheries of Brazil, my outlook changed a little. While I think it is still important that those stories be told, I'm much more interested in finding the contemporary parallels in Shakespeare's works.

During the dictatorial times in Brazil, there was a real push to make a difference with the arts. This lost its way a little and people became more preoccupied about being the best artists, rather than focusing on how the work is still relevant nowadays. This is what prompted me to return to the fundamental question of how possible it was to use the arts to comment on people and society.

Now, my approach is getting closer to the performance, where I work to deconstruct the character and think about the sincerity of the performer on stage, connecting the audience through an emotional approach, and taking them beyond the logical understanding of Shakespeare's works, using images, movement, words, sounds and sensations to do it.

The foundation of my approach

I've worked with lots of companies, and all of them had a different artistic 'language': some of them more theatre, other more circus and dance. When I first arrived in London to work, I didn't speak English very well, so I realized that words in theatre were a kind of boundary. How could I deeply touch people, if they don't understand me?

Then I remembered when I was about 18, and I did a lot of research into the Japanese dance *butoh* and its main dancer Kazuo Ohon, who used to say: 'When you dance *butoh*, you dance with your ghosts, your fears, your happiness, and joy. When you dance *butoh*, you journey back to your mother's womb, and in this journey, you understand better who you are.'

Then I realized that with movement, image and sound there are no boundaries. At this moment I decided my approach to art would be about using the theatre as a space to mix the visual arts, with dance, music and sensations.

During my research into Japanese culture I discovered that, unlike the West, where one is either a singer or an actor or a dancer respectively, in Japan, everything is learnt together. This is what set me off, and what inspired me to create a theatre company where there was no difference between the different disciplines. After working extensively with a contemporary circus group, called Intrepida Trupe, who combine theatre with circus skills, and also the theatre group Nós do Morro, and seeing how many of them also played instruments, I really opened my mind to everything that was possible as an artist. And this was the point: I didn't want to define anyone as an 'actor', they were 'artists' – who could turn their hand to anything. After ten successful years with the company, Cicely Berry visited Brazil, fell in love with Nós do Morro's work, and very kindly invited us to come to the United Kingdom as part of the Complete Works Festival.

My experience with Shakespeare, like many, started at school. As a young professional, when I was 20, I did an open-air, promenade production of *Romeo and Juliet* around a park, where I was Romeo. The next big thing though was the work with the RSC, which really inspired me and reignited that determination I had that art must transform people, as I had learned with Cicely Berry. After returning to Brazil, the very well-received Nós do Morro production of *The Two Gentlemen of Verona* was invited to transfer to the Barbican in 2008.

In Brazil, if you didn't come from a wealthy background, your education was limited, but this wasn't the case in Europe. When I arrived, we started to talk about different skills and how they might work together, and I discovered so much talent. In Europe I could find artists who could dance, play instruments and also deliver well a piece of text.

Work with young people

When Deborah Shaw invited me to work with young people as part of the World Shakespeare Festival and the LIFT Festival, at the Roundhouse, during the London Olympic Games, I wanted to find a way to encourage the young people to express what they wanted to express, in whichever way they found best. The conversation quickly turned to love – it's very strong and everybody can identify with it, it's a universal thing. We discussed it in the context of Hamlet, Othello and Romeo and Juliet – all relationships that don't work out – and we explored the repercussions of love when it loses control. It's incredible, because Shakespeare's stories spoke to his time, and spoke to his society, but they are equally as valid and pertinent now. We tried to investigate these modern connections, by asking what is and who is a contemporary Hamlet? Or a contemporary Romeo and Juliet? Do they even exist anymore? From this discussion emerged our stimulus – the dark side of love.

Our aim was to use all media and all skills to actually create a more accessible and universal piece of theatre that doesn't concern itself so much with narrative, but takes pains over engaging the audience on a personal level with each character.

When I first saw the Javier Bardem film *Biutiful* (2010), I was compelled to research into it. What I found was the director lost his son, when his son was 10 years old, and there was a necessity to talk about his loss – so he did this film. And this was an idea that struck me, which I shared with the young people: when you do something on stage, you do it because you really needed to do it. Don't show us, don't pretend; do it because you really needed to. This idea applied literally, but also in the producing of the work; I wanted to do something that they really wanted to speak about, that they really connected with.

It was quite a difficult process at the beginning, because I was so used to being in Brazil where everything is very open and people share everything, but here in England, people were more reserved – particularly when discussing love. So, we found an entry point, and focused on Hamlet and how, very simply, he becomes overwhelmed with family problems and this affects his relationship with Ophelia – it perturbs his love life. This was a starting point that resonated with people, and from there, they started to share their own stories. This reluctance to share was also true of death, which is the complete antithesis of how it is in Brazil. There, people are exposed to death frequently and quite brutally: whether this is on the street at the scene of an accident, or sensationalist photographs in the newspaper. In Britain, everything is concealed and censored, and death is more of an idea than it is something physical that you can observe. There is so much death in Shakespeare's plays – take the three plays we were discussing, for instance, *Othello*, *Romeo and Juliet* and *Hamlet* – and so it was important that they understood what death was, and what it looked like. So, I asked them to bring pictures in of 'death' – people, or otherwise – and we created a tableau, not necessarily of bodies or anything particularly literal, but a scene of death or bereavement. We asked ourselves, how can we represent death in the theatre? In Brazil we have a market dedicated to selling the possessions of dead people, and I suddenly thought of shoes, because I think shoes are quite personal and evocative. So, I threw a pair of shoes on stage and this was the start point for creating these images, these tableaux. I think an image on stage can touch someone much more profoundly than a page of text, so we built these images up with music, and the simplicity of these everyday scenes, I hope, moved people to reflect on how the situation touched them.

Influences

When I was a teenager, I never went to the theatre, but I loved the cinema because it engulfs you, and gives you that sensation of being inside the story. This is something I have striven to achieve in all my work – particularly the early promenade pieces in Brazil – but is also a reason I combine art forms, to make it as consuming as possible. My research into Japanese culture led me to discover Kazuo Ohon and *butoh* dance, which changed my life because of its insistence on moving to express yourself. The world is so immediate and fast-paced now, and I think that's why the immediate, strong physical images of the cinema and the nature of *butoh* dance are so important, because they cut straight to the emotional response.

I have also always been inspired by the work of the great Peter Brook and Eugenio Barba, and how the diversity of different cultures affected them and their work; their work demonstrates how each culture can bring something different to the artistic process. It was fascinating, and it is what inspired me to travel so much; to explore how different cultures communicate and the way they express their art. In fact, I travelled to India because both Barba and Brook had.

Once, I had the opportunity to meet with Peter Brook. He was emphatic about how research needs to be tested in practice; how essential it is that our questions echo and reverberate fully, and overflow into an image of the wider world, making visible the invisible. So, that is what I've been putting into practice in my work.

Shakespeare inspired me a lot of course, because of the beautiful stories, the beautiful texts, but above all because he wrote these stories that are still relevant today – these things still happen. With Greek tragedy and mythology, you can identify with the moral, the hero, the text possibly, but with Shakespeare, the stories you see still happen. It's funny to say, but I think his words have the same power as a painting, much like *butoh*: it's powerful and deliberate, and everything has a reason, which is embedded in the text. You don't need to colour it with outside influences, it's all there.

CLAIRE VAN KAMPEN, SENIOR RESEARCH FELLOW AND FOUNDING DIRECTOR OF MUSIC, SHAKESPEARE'S GLOBE

Once you've created work at the Globe, you realize the extent to which the playwright was writing *for* that space, and also for Middle Temple Hall, and for the Blackfriars. These different spaces have some important things in common: they don't have a lighting vocabulary, and they don't have amplified sound, so, whether you're in Shakespeare's indoor theatre, a large hall or his outdoor amphitheatre, the actors and audience are in one 'world', in one space, together. For this reason, the music you write for a Shakespeare play has to be inclusive, and it has to be understood by the audience, on a deep, experiential level.

Composing for a production originating in a modern space – for example, a West End theatre, when the entire audience is seated, and usually in darkness – without prior knowledge of composing for the unique dynamic of Elizabethan and Jacobean playhouses is like trying to unlearn what you know. To return to the idea of this notional modern dress production in the West End, given what I know about what works so beautifully at the Globe and the Sam Wanamaker Playhouse, I would probably leave the houselights on the audience for much of the time, if not all of the time, so that the audience knew that they could be seen by the actors.

These days, I feel just as familiar with the Wanamaker as I do with the Globe; I opened the Wanamaker – the indoor companion to the outdoor amphitheatre of the Globe – and since have been able to learn the same kind of things in that space as I had learned at the Globe. What I learned was that the spaces were in fact not all that different, and that having a roof on a building doesn't really change your attitude to the work: you're not telling the audience something, you're not showing them something, you're not doing something *for* them, you're doing something *with* them and experiencing the play together.

For this reason, your musical choices have to be very grounded, and they must be understood by the audience. Whatever you choose to do, it is a language that the audience has to be part of: it can't be mystifying, and it can't draw attention to itself in ways that occlude Shakespeare's text. Music shouldn't be employed as 'soundtrack' in Shakespeare.

Shakespeare's text never becomes sentimental, and so you (should) strive to take all of the sentiment out of the way you speak and stage the text, because you want the audience – not the people on stage – to be going on that emotional journey. Shakespeare's text doesn't ooze sentimental description, and you have to honour that with the music. There is no point in creating a tautology, having (for example) angst-ridden music underscoring Claudius's speech 'O, my offence is rank' (*Hamlet*, 3.3.36–72). And yet, more often than not, that is what happens, and when this happens the music is not in service of the play, but in service of the director.

Such an approach is appropriate for filmmaking, but our film culture has done a great disservice to Shakespeare in the theatre. Instead of overlapping the end of one scene with the beginning of the next one – this 'handing over of the baton' is usually signalled clearly by a rhyming couplet – the norm has become instead a soundtrack, which holds together music, sound, lighting changes and unnecessarily lengthy and complex scene changes. Music can serve a different, important purpose: even if you do scene changes which are seamless, often you will need help to go from one location to another. For example, in *Measure for Measure*, you will help to get from the Duke's quarters, to the Convent, to just outside the prison gates and so on. Music can provide a simple marker – as simple as a bell ringing, perhaps – to help in this way … But what you *don't* need is a lot of emotional description. You don't need *any* of that, in that play … ever!

This is where my job as composer, working with a director, can sometimes get tricky. In most cases, a director will want to underscore Isabella's soliloquy 'To whom should I complain?' (*Measure for Measure*, 2.4.170–86), either to make the speech more plaintive, or to make us more sympathetic to her. Because music is *always* more powerful than text, our ears will immediately be drawn to the musical underscoring, and instead of the specificity of her words, you will hear only an emotional wash, and the generality of her speech. This is why I think you need to take all underscoring, all 'emotional comment' out of any Shakespeare play, and let the words do it.

Another reason music doesn't typically work in combination with spoken text is that verse has a different rhythm all its own. There are rare instances when you can use music as an interesting rhythmic antithesis to the text; *Richard II* is a case in point. Shakespeare knows about musical antithesis: he writes music into the Act 5 scene where Richard is in prison (*Richard II*, 5.5). The music in that scene feeds a whole series of Richard's comments about time, and how he can't control time, or even music, anymore, because he is now in the position of a humble beggar, a prisoner. He speaks a phrase with multiple layers of meaning – 'Ha, ha, keep time!' (42) – and the whole speech (5.5.1–66) is constructed with that music in mind … it isn't a director's idea, it's Shakespeare's idea, and it is remarkable … not typical.

Another remarkable way in which Shakespeare uses music is in *A Midsummer Night's Dream*, when Titania and Oberon call for music 'such as charmeth sleep' (4.1.82): and, as is the case with the scene I just mentioned from *Richard II*, there is no 'out-point' for the music indicated. What does that mean? Does it mean it was arbitrary in Shakespeare's day? Did they stop at different places? Did they do what we do, which is just sort of fade out? Where elsewhere stage directions are so specific, why didn't Shakespeare indicate where the music stops? He doesn't indicate musicians coming on stage, as he does in *Romeo and Juliet* … it's very strange. One potential answer might seem very odd for a modern audience, one used to being able to obtain any kind of music, whenever it wants to; I think that an Elizabethan audience, given the chance to listen to some beautiful music, perhaps something played on a bass viol, would not have wanted to listen to anything *else* over the top of that music.

I think it is entirely possible that the audience stood and listened to an entire piece of music here, almost like an entr'act. The text doesn't stipulate that it is played offstage, so it could well have been played from the gallery, or indeed from onstage, because there is a scene-change taking place: it is very likely that the doubling scheme used had the same actors playing Hippolyta/Titania and Theseus/Oberon, so those actors needed a change of clothing at this point. And, whereas a modern audience might wonder why the scene change is being held up, an Elizabethan audience might well have had an appreciation for a piece of music at this juncture of the play (possibly played on a bass lute and a tenor viol) as a wonderful ending to the whole journey of Titania and Oberon: Harmonia has been brought in, between Mars and Venus (who have been in strife) and made everything good between them. I think the function of music – particularly in *Dream* – is very easily misunderstood. In postwar Rodgers and Hammerstein musicals – we'll use *South Pacific* as an example – we are quite happy to sit and listen to the whole of 'Some Enchanted Evening' because the song takes us to a different place by the end of it, from where we began. The song is the vehicle that moves us forward, in terms of understanding the characters and their narrative. Now why could that not have been the case for *A Midsummer Night's Dream*?

Film culture has made music too subservient, characterless and, at the same time, infuriatingly 'in the way'. Music has not yet been given its proper place in Shakespeare, as part of the narrative culture of the play. Our film culture has infected our perception of music in that regard: for us, music is 'background', but examples of background music in Elizabethan culture are very rare indeed. Normally, they will dance to it, talk about it (as with the example from *Richard II*), but the first evidence of 'piped in' music comes from the court of King Christian of Denmark … who was OCD and couldn't bear to see musicians playing instruments, and so he kept his musicians in horrible dank conditions down in a basement, from which he had pipes going up into his room so the music could be 'piped in'. We know this because Dowland was one of those musicians who earned a lot of money writing for King Christian, despite the fact that the king couldn't bear looking at him! But this is a real anomaly, and as such, tells us a lot about Shakespeare's use of music.

If you use music unknowingly, or carelessly, you destroy that very particular power of music, which Shakespeare absolutely understood, and knew how to use. So, as a composer, once you've 'been there', and understood these things, you can't unlearn them. Let's be clear: it isn't necessary to use music of Shakespeare's period. Music from any period can be used, as long as the audience understands why it's there. You might use a fantastic contemporary ballad where the text might suggest 'heavenly' music for bass lute and tenor viol, if that ballad has an equivalent 'heavenly' effect on a contemporary audience. That might be the better choice, as long as the audience understands what the music is *doing* … and if they *don't*, it shouldn't be there.

A composer doesn't need to replicate what the text is doing, because the text does it so well. The situations in Shakespeare's plays are not difficult to understand today – we still fall in love, we still go to war, we still feel hatred or fear – and so if the actor really understands what they are saying, and really feels that need to speak, there is no reason to slather music all over the text in order to tell a modern audience what is going on. The challenge for a composer is to get your ego out of the way, because often, as a musician, when the text is moving, you hear certain music in response to that, but you have to resist putting that music into a Shakespeare play. Sometimes it is too easy to persuade a director that a piece of music will really enhance a speech or scene – *mea culpa*! I have done this myself – and, if you've chosen a beautiful piece played on a beautiful instrument, they will be so drawn to 'that moment' that you forget that, in fact, you have together taken away 'that moment' from the actor, and denied the audience the opportunity to really hear the language, and to really understand it.

If we could treat Shakespeare's dramaturgy as though it were modern, fresh on the page, we might be inclined to show more respect for the plays as written, but we are stuck in a culture where directors are under pressure to 'do something' with Shakespeare plays, to be inventive with it, because the critics are coming to *see what you will do with it*. It's difficult to imagine this urge to *do something with* a modern playwright's work, but because Shakespeare has been dead for 400 years, it's increasingly difficult for directors to resist these pressures. Sadly, these conceits and interventions just put up barriers between the actor and the audience. In the case of *Hamlet*, a choice to underscore those famous soliloquies will remove Hamlet from the shared space with the audience, and put him 'in his own world', as though in a film, and as a result it becomes impossible to build that empathy between the actor and the audience … and why would you want to do that?

These days, my instincts are to have absolutely no music at all once the play has begun, other than what is specified in the texts themselves. Why would you need it?

SIAN WILLIAMS, CHOREOGRAPHER

My first point of contact with a Shakespeare play is usually a brief conversation with the director who has invited me to work on the production ... this will cover what they are thinking of, in broad terms, for their production. And then I will read the play, and get to know it, if I am not already familiar with it. It varies, but sometimes I have a set of questions that I need to ask the director, in order to find out what it is they want from me. Other times, the director has a very clear vision of what they're wanting, so they will be more prescriptive from the outset.

I'm always keen to try and understand if they are wanting something from 'within' the play – because Shakespeare gives clear stage directions for dance, and then you know that there is what we might call a conventional dance of that period happening – or, if it is a more modern production, it might be some version of a social dance as well as movement direction – so sometimes it'll be self-evident.

But, for example, I worked on *Love's Labour's Lost* with Dominic Dromgoole here [at the Globe], and Dominic wanted some little 'inserts' if you like, little linking-scenes, that he knew he wanted to be danced. I needed to be clear that he wanted something moving to music in a kind of stylized fashion, as opposed to maybe a more abstract thing, so there was a little bit of discussion as to what that might be. He had a very clear picture of the women doing a 'pre-hunting' dance, and so we worked on that, and it was nicely evocative, sort of a prelude to the speech that the Princess makes about death (*Love's Labour's Lost*, 4.1.21–35). For this kind of thing, fact-finding becomes very important, and I really enjoy those tasks which are quite married to the drama of the story.

Research

I also like to listen to the kind of music that might be 'in the right vein' for the production, because the composer might be creating his or her own music, or be inspired by something from the period, and I listen to something of that particular period to get the feel of it. Working a lot on Shakespeare, I've become quite familiar with medieval music, for example, but it is always nice to be given suggestions of pieces from the composer. Often they're inspired by something much more ancient; I recently worked with somebody who worked with ancient Scandinavian folk dance music, and with the wonders of the computer nowadays I was easily able to access that sort of thing. And (for the same reason) I *love* using YouTube, because there is an *amazing* amount of folk dance on there, including clips of traditional dances that you can see have been passed on down the ages, with senior and junior members of the community dancing together. These are sometimes amateurish versions, of course, but they are fantastic because they give you a good sense of what the dance represents to those people. And, of course, there are professional level dancers on YouTube as well. There's loads of material available, it is fascinating and it gives you a way in to understanding bodies moving together in a particular style.

Sometimes I get very specific details from this material. For instance, although all folk dances across Europe have got certain qualities that are linked, you will find some really interesting unique features. For a *Much Ado About Nothing* I worked on, the composer wanted to work with a Moroccan feeling to the music, because they were setting it in Sicily with migratory links to North Africa. So again, I research what's still going on in the way of music and dance in those countries and this feeds into what I choreograph. It frees me up when I can see that people are making contemporary their own traditional dances. This stops me from being slavish, prevents me from getting stuck in some sort of cod idea of the thing; I remember that I have to make it *my* own choreography, as well, and bring it into this living theatre. So, I bring my own idea to something that I can find out about through research, for example, dance patterns that might look familiar to someone who comes from Morocco (as something drawn from their traditional dance) but it also has a twist.

I find the democracy of what the computer has done is amazing for research. I've got books that are wonderful, that give me historical information, and the notation of things, but what people are putting into 'people's channels' is really thrilling. Of course, you have to sort through this material, and decide what it is that you're taking from them, but it is fascinating.

Once I did a dance based on lateral thinking, because the director (Tim Carroll) wanted something with a kind of *Stomp*-ish, heavy-footed, regimented feel to it. I just put 'boot dance' into YouTube, which I thought might come up with some kind of marching dance. And this LA kind of street dancing came up, which had a very rootsy feel. In it I saw lots of connections to different folk dances but with more edginess to it. This was a fantastic inspiration I was able to use.

The jigs at the Globe

I have the great privilege of working on 'the jig' at the Globe; we invariably have a dance at the end of the show, because research shows that they had such a thing habitually [in Shakespeare's time] whether the show was a tragedy or a comedy. Because I have done so many of these I have developed a process that I find very helpful. The jig has to serve various functions: at the end of the show some catharsis is required, to bring us back to reality; sometimes it's very nice to linger a while on what you've just seen. Sometimes you want to bring about a kind of crescendo … various things need to be orchestrated. Another requirement of the jig is to involve the whole company who have presented this story and let them celebrate their union with you – the audience. So there are various things which need to happen, including, for the actors, to take in all of the audience and acknowledge them all, in this unique space.

I'll need to know what the director would like to achieve from the jig, whether that is just a kind of short, sharp burst of energy, or a little parody of what has been going on in the play, with characters from the play having a bit of fun at their own expense. So I gather that information. Most often the composer already knows what they're going to do for the jig, because they have had a separate discussion with the director, and they have an overview of what is required from them throughout the piece.

If the music comes first, I like to listen to it and sort of 'dance-dream', or play around with it – in my kitchen! – moving to it and sort of feeling what the rhythm suggests. I usually like to come up with a few movement phrases that might work, and to think about the overall structure: I might want to begin with everyone arriving on stage together, or have the rest of the company join those who are already on stage at the end of the play. Then I might think about how certain actors make contact with others on stage, and then take their gaze out to the audience to make contact with them.

There are some very simple transactions or 'little essences' which are part of the kaleidoscope of the whole dance, and I like to think of these independently, at first, rather than getting myself bogged down by thinking about how this or that bigger pattern has to happen. If I have the luxury of a few sessions with the actors, I like to begin by introducing these simple transactions, and having fun with the company trying out ideas; invariably the actors will take this information and come back with a little bit more; they're great at improvising, and finding things which offer even more possibilities. In one of the recent sessions I liked the idea of using scarves, in a chaotic and comedic way, so I got them to improvise in different partnerships and configurations, and the results were hilarious. We created a section in the dance that was made by the actors through these improvisations.

Having a little bit of time to generate these ideas in the first session means that on the second and third session I'm basically making those ideas work within patterns or templates that work with the space, which you need when you have twenty or so people on the stage. And of course I am influenced by the director; though this is a very familiar process for me now, and as much as I have my own ideas, I have to be sure these aren't out of line with what the director is hoping to see.

Flamenco and other influences

I had an eclectic training, comprising lots of techniques, rather than pure ballet, or a single contemporary dance style. I did historic dance, for example, but in conjunction with jazz, Graham and Cunningham technique, ballet and social dance – at the time I thought ballroom dancing might not prove that useful – however, I have found it incredibly informative over the years. We may be accustomed to thinking of face-to-face dancing only in terms of classic waltzes and other sorts of ballroom dancing, but in fact it goes back much further than that. The function of that connection – dancing face to face, looking into your partner's eyes and holding hands – is very deep, and I draw on my study of that all the time, I go towards it quite readily. Dances found in a Shakespeare text generally work on the basis of having a partner, and there are references to ancient circle dances, which go back even further. All of my initial training seems to keep informing what I do now.

I did flamenco dance as a hobby, for a long time, and I've always enjoyed using the rhythms of flamenco, which I find so attractive, almost intoxicating. Flamenco is based on some quite simple elements, put together in complex ways; clapping and stamping are quite fundamental things in the Globe space, and I've drawn on those elements a lot. If you have knowledge in this area you'd recognize the way I've used flamenco's syncopated clapping and stamping in that space.

For me, it's less important that everyone looks like expert dancers: the rhythm we are working with is important and has to be consistent, but I believe it is crucial for actors to feel as though they own the dance they are doing, that it doesn't seem imposed on them in any way. It shouldn't be a precocious display of skill – although it *is* skilful – but it should have a kind of natural *gusto* to it, with the company letting their hair down a bit. In common with the flamenco philosophy, the dance they do is seen as a gift for the audience. It's not a performance as such, but a gift that welcomes and inspires the audience, hopefully making them feel as though they could (almost) get up and join in. Dance shouldn't be rarefied, in my view, especially dance in the theatre: you should feel a human connection with it. Having said that, the companies tend to overcome any initial shyness quite quickly, and become quite keen to get the jigs as technically precise as they can, because it will please their audience; the more masterful they become, the more they are able to enjoy it, and share it with the audience. The great thing about working with actors is that once they start to feel at home with the moves, they start to personalize them in a lovely way, as though it is the character from the play who is doing the jig; it's important to be able to respond to the physicality they are building for the character and incorporate it into the jig.

The technical demands of the Globe space

Glynn Macdonald has worked at the Globe for a long time, and she understands it so beautifully. She is an Alexander Technique specialist and has a fantastic understanding of bodies in space – the air around you, the earth beneath you, the sky above you – and she also has a wonderfully holistic understanding of how bodies reflect the social structures, in terms of status and bearing, how that is affected by people's perception of their position in life. She uses this to guide the movement work of the actors, beginning with the expectation of honesty in movement that comes hand in hand with working in shared light. That's not to say that when you are being lit you are not being 'honest', but working in shared light in that space I feel makes you very focused on what your every fibre is conveying. Actors' bodies are never 'background' at the Globe, and you can't afford to 'switch off' at any point. You are always very near somebody, even if you are right at the 'back'. This is something you have to embrace, because it is undeniable, even down to the things like catching an audience member's eye because their small child has hold of your dress and is exploring the texture of the velvet ... for these reasons it is exhilarating to perform at the Globe, and I love that at any point you can read the story through the bodies and bearing of the people who aren't even speaking.

Roots and influences

I couldn't do the work I do anywhere else without the work I do with The Kosh: this is the most challenging work I do. It is devised, which often begins from something as small as a synopsis of a story, or a theme. Devising with The Kosh allows for some deep exploration, discovering how people build stories and respond to different imaginative stimuli. This is very helpful indeed for everything else I do. There is inevitable, necessary repetition in what's required for a Shakespeare play so it's lovely to have something else that can refresh and nourish this 'regular' work by giving you insights into the different ways people respond to information and new stories.

Another thing I love about devising is the opportunity it gives me to narrow the focus and work on one particular aspect. That might be something as simple as wanting to find all the ways there are to sit at a table, and from an initial exploration develop a movement sequence to help us remember all of that material. From there, we give ourselves a new piece of information, which might be much more about the psychology of the scene, but we'll impose the restriction of exploring that new piece of information using only the movements we have already learned. Self-imposed limitation can actually be quite liberating, because you find your movements differently motivated from the way you might have expected, in ways that disrupt the conventional. Whether it is a case of using verse to find freedom in speaking, or using learned movement patterns to find physical freedom, using structure to find freedom is always exciting.

Conclusions

I am inspired by what Geraldine Collinge says about 'change': in her role as director of events at the Royal Shakespeare Company she is charged with expanding the range of stakeholders in the company, 'breaking down traditional barriers, bringing people closer to Shakespeare, changing people's perceptions of Shakespeare and changing their relationship with Shakespeare' (p. 112). Citing local and national initiatives, and in particular her team's work with large-scale campaigns using digital platforms, such as 'Such Tweet Sorrow' in 2010 (a modern, loose adaptation of *Romeo and Juliet* performed on Twitter over five weeks via a series of tweets from six RSC actors), Geraldine presents the RSC's commitment to 'a big brand-change ... a big shift in what people expected of the RSC' (p. 113). In turn, this prompts me to consider how the interviews with actors and creatives as a whole reflect the extent to which Shakespeare – or the way we *make* Shakespeare today – is changing.

The living tradition

For various reasons which this section will consider, the interviews suggest that theatre practice within the larger Shakespeare-producing houses evolves rather slowly. Listening to the respondents, I found it possible to trace what the late

Peter Hall once described as a 'living tradition' of mainstream practice with a common approach to acting, verse-speaking and directing Shakespeare's plays. It may further surprise the reader to learn that the two books with which the respondents find themselves most in dialogue are *On Directing Shakespeare* by Ralph Berry (published in 1989) and *Playing Shakespeare* by the late John Barton (published in 1984). This is not to suggest a kind of stagnation within the industry, far from it: Shakespeare's plays represent unparalleled creative opportunities for the actors, designers and directors working in every corner of the globe. What the interviews do suggest, however, is that theatre practice is fundamentally different from literary-critical responses to the plays: by its very nature, literary criticism is responsive not just to the plays, but to the plays as read in a constantly changing political, cultural, social context; conversely, practice, by its nature, is refreshed and adapted, rather than overhauled or rejected, in a pragmatic way. As I suggest in the Introduction, the teachings of Stanislavski, first published in English in 1936, continue to underpin modern actor training, sometimes explicitly, sometimes in different guises, as if to imply 'if it ain't broke . . .'

John Barton (1928–2018) and his legacy: 'playing Shakespeare' then and now

The interviews in this book suggest strongly that there are at least three generations of actors in the United States and the United Kingdom who share a common understanding and set of shared practices with regard to speaking Shakespeare's verse. This common ground can be traced in the first instance to a 1982 series of groundbreaking TV broadcasts, in which John Barton worked with a company of eminent RSC actors in verse workshops, in the series for LWTV/Channel 4, *Playing Shakespeare*. The programmes, which are now globally accessible via YouTube, and the continuing popularity of the accompanying paperback which transcribes the workshops (now in its second edition with a CD of the TV series) have facilitated the continuing and widespread dissemination of Barton's techniques in drama schools.

Of course, nothing comes from nothing, and there are older principles and teachings which inform Barton's work, and these can be traced to his own training at Cambridge, under the tutelage of George 'Dadie' Rylands. I would be foolish to argue that nothing has changed within 'mainstream' Shakespeare production since Barton and Berry published their books in the 1980s, but nonetheless the interviews, and my own experience as a director and teacher of acting on both sides of the Atlantic suggest that for actors and creatives working today, the opportunities, challenges and provocations associated with the production of Shakespeare's plays continue to be articulated using paradigms that Berry and Barton may legitimately claim to have coined over thirty years ago. This discussion attempts to trace this lineage in broad terms, and to reveal the 'patterns in the wallpaper' which connect the thirty respondents in this volume.

Two traditions: then and now

In 1982, with the popular LWT series for Channel 4, *Playing Shakespeare,* John Barton suggested that to play Shakespeare successfully on the modern stage was to marry together 'two traditions' – these traditions were actually what might be described as potentially competing concerns for the demands of (on the one hand) 'heightened language' and (on the other) 'naturalism' in performance. The latter concept can be traced to the teaching and philosophy of Stanislavski, while the metaphor of balance between naturalism and heightened language has its origins in the teaching practice of George Rylands, the Cambridge University tutor who mentored Barton, as well as Peter Hall and Trevor Nunn, among others.

Abigail Rokison (2009) notes that Rylands himself was influenced by the work of William Poel, who favoured bare stages and championed close attention to verse speaking in his productions of Shakespeare plays; perhaps for these reasons, Poel is by turns credited and/or blamed for coining the idea of 'authenticity' in approaches to Shakespeare. Rokison reminds us that '[o]ne can see in Poel's assertions the origins of the concern with the recovery of Shakespeare's "intention" which is central to the modern approach to textual analysis and delivery' (Rokison, 2009, 30). The William Poel Memorial Prize was instituted at RADA in 1973 by the Society for Theatre Research 'for the speaking of dramatic verse or prose at a competition held at the Royal Academy of Dramatic Art' (Anon., 1973), and certainly Poel's rigour and aesthetic proved hugely influential, not least because they informed Rylands, and so subsequently, generations of Rylands's students. So, as historic genealogies go, Poel's is an influential one, but it was Rylands's students who were responsible for bringing this quest for authorial clues in the text and for 'authenticity' in verse speaking onto the public stages of the RSC and the National Theatre. Once Rylands's student Barton had brought these ideas to popular television, in the series of programmes for *Playing Shakespeare*, introduced by Barton's friend and Cambridge colleague Trevor Nunn, they were adopted as an industry and pedagogic standard.

Barton died in January 2018, before this volume's publication, but his place within the Shakespeare industry remains absolutely central. His work is cited frequently in this volume, as a succession of actors and directors relate their own position – on verse speaking in particular – to his. Barton continued to run workshops to RSC actors until 2016, and his approach to verse has been generally adopted by the RSC verse and text coaches who support the work of the directors of productions of Shakespeare. Ankur Bahl describes how he was encouraged 'to learn and develop as an actor, a performer, and a Shakespearean' (an interesting appropriation of musical theatre's 'triple-threat' concept) with the help of '[v]ocal coaches, accent coaches, people who wanted to talk about rhetoric, people who wanted to look at the text and break it down, other actors who had done it tons of times before and were more than willing to help' (p. 25). Despite the impressive resources deployed in reinforcing Barton's work, it is difficult to say whether Barton's practice has been developed, adapted, expanded or diluted, in the process of being handed down; the difficulty lies in the metaphor of balance that is at the core of Barton's practice. Barton's somewhat flexible concept of balancing technique with truthfulness (in the sense of a post-Stanislavskian understanding of naturalism) is of course very open to interpretation and matters of taste. I would argue that tastes, rather than practices, have shifted over the past thirty-some years, and, with the popularity of verbatim theatre, and increased emphasis on screen acting in most drama schools, the twenty-first-century drama school graduate will perhaps interpret 'heightened language' and 'naturalness' differently from Barton and Hall, and their RSC companies of the 1970s and 1980s, who would have graduated some fifty years ago. Likewise, technical rigor may be judged differently, and so the same balance between these Bartonian concepts may produce speech in young actors today which sounds quite unlike recordings of Barton's advocates Judi Dench, Ian McKellen et al. made in the 1970s and 1980s, despite the same basic principles being at the core of the training then as now.

Indeed, if we are to speak of 'two traditions' within actor training at this precise moment in time, and ask how these relate to the UK Shakespeare industry today, we might instead find that we are talking as much about casting and professional development as we are about performance styles. The route from drama school to the RSC or West End, it might be argued, has developed a major diversion more recently. The experience of many recent drama school graduates is that they are more likely to be offered roles at the RSC, the Globe and elsewhere, if they have first established themselves as screen actors, on film or television. Agents representing newly graduated or young actors will, given a choice, steer their clients more towards film and television castings, because the pay is higher in this sector, and so are the rates of commission. Most London agents charge about 12.5 per cent commission for theatre work, but will take between 15 and 20 per cent of their client's wage for screen work in films, television or commercials. Screen acting is taught in drama schools with an emphasis on internalized physical choices, heavy reliance on subtext, use of the so-called inner monologue, and in these and other ways, the approach to teaching screen acting differs so radically from the way actors continue to be taught how to use blank verse or 'heightened language', that the professed connection between success on the small screen and a part on the bigger stage is curious, counterintuitive and, in my opinion, quite troubling.

The same trend may be seen in those young actors who work outside the parameters of a drama school training, in that they 'are more likely to have served an apprenticeship in television drama before tackling Shakespearean texts' (Rokison, 2009, 9–10).

At the level of local detail, for the actors I interviewed, the concept of 'two traditions' seems most useful as a description of two general approaches to the related concepts of enjambment and caesurae. Actors who identify themselves as verse-focused will emphasize the need to do 'something' with the verse line endings: Andrew Long notes that he can 'hear the sense of the speech just by saying the first and last stress of each line' (p. 60), and Jade Anouka remembers an exercise that 'really showed me that, in fact, line endings were my friend' (p. 22). Actors who profess themselves to be more relaxed about really using the verse 'correctly' will tend to prioritize phrasing which keeps thoughts unbroken, and which consequently may involve enjambment ('running on') and pausing at the midline caesurae.

We can trace this bifurcation back to the influence of Peter Hall. As mentioned above, Hall was, like Barton, a student of Rylands at Cambridge, and like Rylands he advocates close examination of the metrical qualities of Shakespeare's verse, and attentiveness to the shifts in rhythm, tempo and dynamic, as a means of mining the text for authorial indications of 'authentic' verse speaking. Hall's collaboration with John Barton is obliquely referred to by many in this book, and in these accounts Hall is usually depicted as the hardliner on marking the ends of verse lines, while Barton's approach appears more flexible in the workshops broadcast in the 'Playing Shakespeare' series, linking the impulse to run-on (enjambment) or take midline pauses with the quest for naturalness which is a part of 'our modern tradition' of acting.

If Barton's work still represents RSC practice, Hall's legacy has had more exposure at the Globe in the past twenty years, thanks to the work of Giles Block (the Globe's Master of the Words, and Hall's former associate director) and Tim Carroll, a self-professed 'even-more-rigorous Peter Hall' (p. 105). Giles Block's long tenure at the Globe – spanning four artistic directorships, from 1999 to the present – has ensured that many hundreds of actors have been coached in the 'Globe style' of verse speaking which owes much to Hall's faith in the embedded authorial intention hidden in (or revealed by) the structure of the verse. Block finds line endings particularly leading in this regard, and he argues in *Speaking the Speech* that 'Shakespeare is able to bring out the precise meaning his characters are aiming at, by what he chooses to put at the end of the line' (2013, 24). Giles's excellent book has been widely adopted in drama schools in the United Kingdom, and his practical work as a director at the American Shakespeare Center's Blackfriars Playhouse has increased his influence as a verse 'guru' on both sides of the Atlantic. Tim Carroll founded The Factory with actor Alex Hassell, and their interviews in this volume draw the same conclusions as Hall (2014, 5) does as he describes with conviction and confidence the 'living tradition' of verse speaking to which he belongs: 'What Shakespeare demands always works. And his notation is amazingly accurate'.

Two traditions: 'here' and 'there'?

In the United States, the line between the 'two traditions' seems to be even more sharply drawn, and metaphors of balance seem less applicable. Stanislavski's system, though undoubtedly still dominant within UK actor training institutions, may be said almost to monopolize actor training institutions in the United States. American acting, and perhaps screen acting to an even greater degree, has embraced Stanislavski's system and, controversially, made it its own. Many actor trainers working in the United States would argue that for American actors, 'two traditions' in performing Shakespeare might in fact refer to, on the one hand, a 'British tradition' (summarized above) and, on the other, an 'American' approach, borrowed from Moscow and developed in New York City.

The American Laboratory Theatre in New York City is arguably the spiritual home of American acting. It was established in 1923 by Richard Boleslavsky and Maria Ouspenskaya, who were part of Stanislavski's famous Moscow Art Theatre company, which toured the United States and Europe in 1922. Of the hundreds of students who enrolled for classes at the Lab (as it was then called), Harold Clurman and Lee Strasberg went on to form the highly influential Group Theatre with Cheryl Crawford in 1931. The Group Theatre's company members included Stella Adler and Sanford Meisner, and the Group's first summer training and rehearsal programme launched a specific and highly influential acting methodology, based on the teachings of Stanislavski, but taught with the American acting industry very much in mind. The Group's formation was followed by the publication of the first American translation of Stanislavski's *An Actor Prepares* in 1936. The verse coach, director and actor trainer Scott Kaiser reminds us that *An Actor Prepares*, widely regarded as the 'bible' of naturalistic acting, outlines only the first part of Stanislavski's theory of psycho-physical actions, emphasizing the psychological aspect of the craft, through such key concepts as imagination, objectives and use of emotional memory (Kaiser, 2003). *An Actor Prepares* places little emphasis on physical characterization, diction and vocal expressivity in performing Shakespeare, as these elements were addressed in *Building a Character*, published later, in 1949. Merlin (2011) argues that Stanislavsky intended the content in *An Actor Prepares* and *Building a Character* to be published as a single comprehensive volume, but as Kaiser (2003, xv) rightly notes, the gap between Stanislavski's first publication and his second had enormous and lasting consequences for actor training in America: 'Because by 1949, it was already too late. The roots of American psychological realism were firmly embedded in the soil of the American stage. The Group Theatre had already come and gone. The Actor's Studio had already been founded. Marlon Brando had already appeared on Broadway in *A Streetcar Named Desire*. And "the classics" were doomed.' In their place was Lee Strasberg's Method, adapted from Stanislavski's first book and the practice of Vakhtangov, which emphasizes 'affective memory, which means memory of sensation, memory of emotion' (Strasberg, 1969). Highly influential though it was to several generations of American screen actors, Strasberg's Method has by now been discredited by most UK actor training institutions, and it is more generally acknowledged in US conservatoires as a partial and imbalanced representation of Stanislavski's system. Nonetheless, Kaiser (2003, xv) is right to complain that 'while *An Actor Prepares* is still required reading for most Intro to Acting classes in the United States, *Building a Character* is still sorely neglected', leaving American actors in training in the dark about Stanislavski's concern for 'movement, voice, diction, words, phrasing, intonation, rhythm, tempo, accentuation, pausing, intelligibility, volume, tone, punctuation, vowels, consonants, standard speech, verse, scansion, rhetoric – all of the same things that Barton, Berry, and Rodenburg talk about in their books'. Looking at the interviews in this volume, it is easy to detect the continued importance of Barton, Cicely Berry and Patsy Rodenburg's approach to voice, as well as, in a few instances, an underlying perception that actors occasionally have to choose between what feels 'truthful', and what feels 'correct'. With fewer American respondents overall, I have scant evidence from which to draw too many hard and fast conclusions about the differences between US and UK actor training systems, both of which rest on Stanislavskian foundations, but Kaiser's argument is convincing, and his mission – both in print and in practice – to connect Shakespeare and Stanislavski is compelling.

On directing Shakespeare

At this point it seems prudent to give some consideration to the work of directors and other creatives, with a view to tracing similar 'patterns in the wallpaper' that connect creatives from different disciplines within the modern ensemble.

Ralph Berry's *On Directing Shakespeare* identifies four different strategies a director may adopt when staging a Shakespeare play, and uses these to contextualize a wealth of primary evidence in the form of interviews with prominent directors of Shakespeare. The choice of settings Berry (1989, 14–20) names are: (i) Renaissance (in which the period referred to in the play is also reflected in clothing and setting), (ii) Modern (using present-day clothing and setting), (iii) Period analogue (the choice of another historical period other than Renaissance or present) and (iv) Eclectic (which combines costume choices from different periods in history into a single production). In this volume, Ethan McSweeny argues that Berry's formula still has currency today, and throughout this volume other creatives echo Berry's theme. Designer Bunny Christie describes her first point of contact with a director in very similar terms: 'I will talk to the director, and we may decide the world we are interested in, and what era we want to set the play in' (p. 109); and another designer, Tom Piper, goes further, equating Berry's model with 'interpretation' in its broadest sense:

[W]ith Shakespeare the big decision is the whole issue of period, that is, where we are going to set it, and when. No matter how you try to avoid it, basically every act of putting a Shakespeare play on stage is an interpretation, even if you decide that the actors are just going to stand there in their ordinary clothes. (p. 150)

Clothes signify a period in time and often a location, specific or general, and so in Tom Piper's view, 'ordinary clothes' are by no means period-neutral. Tim Carroll's answer to the question of 'where and when' is of course strongly influenced by his experience of working at the Globe on several 'original practices' (OP) productions, the most famous of which is, arguably, his *Twelfth Night* of 2002 (revived in 2013).

When I directed *Twelfth Night,* my objective was to make the 'purest' original practices thing I could make, because original practices save you all the time that you would otherwise spend trying to work out how to make an equivalent of yellow stockings, or how to make an equivalent of cross-gartering, because you *have* yellow stockings, cross-gartered. The enormous simplicity of that means you can get onto the play very quickly. (p. 108; emphasis in the original)

The argument for choosing a visual scheme that is directly suggested by the text is a strong one, but what Tim Carroll reads as the 'enormous simplicity' of OP is of course, not uncontroversial, and, to pick up Tom Piper's point again, neither is OP a 'concept-free' approach. Discussions in the press and within the subject area of Shakespeare Studies have debated at considerable length the artistic and gender politics of (in particular) all-male casts for Globe OP productions, and Tim's argument that adopting OP as a means of focusing on the play alone is equally well-rehearsed, though its most direct expression may be found in the archive of Giles Block's 2000 production of *Hamlet*, which was not strictly speaking an OP production, by virtue of Block casting women in the female roles. As I documented at the time, designer Jenny Tiramani and Block opted for 'modern dress circa 1600' after considering all four of the routes outlined by Berry:

> The decision facing the creative team was whether to translate *Hamlet* in modern dress, into another period in history, into its 'own world', or to experiment with original clothing. The team wanted to avoid the popular cliché image of Hamlet in a ruff holding a skull, as this was felt to be too remote from the audience at the new Globe in 2000. The team accepted that in 1600, the first production of *Hamlet* would have been in modern dress, but in 2000 how do we depict 'dread royalty', and make this read as something other than 'men in suits'? *Hamlet* in a different period in history might involve self-conscious design choices, and distance the audience from the story. *Hamlet* in an 'own world' (ahistorical) setting was unappealing for the same reasons. Without elaborate sets, lighting and amplified sound, storytelling is paramount … the creative team opted for 'modern dress circa 1600'. The play fitted the world of the stage, and it was hoped that this would highlight not individual design choices, but the story in general. (Bessell, 2001)

The creative team for the 2000 Globe *Hamlet* were not arguing that a Jacobean clothing scheme would be more 'authentic', but were consciously trying to avoid the kinds of 'self-conscious design choices' described above by their Globe colleague, Tim Carroll.

Polly Findlay believes that this model is changing, and that a new wave of directors and designers of Shakespeare are beginning their work on the plays from a different perspective. In her interview, Polly describes the process of arriving at design choices for *As You Like It* after considering the social function or *gesture* of the play, at the time it was written, and considering how to replicate that function in the present:

What we ended up thinking was that the nature of the magic in the forest was precisely the same as the nature of the magic in the theatre, in that, if I say to you in a theatre: 'this iPhone is a baby', as long as the nature of that contract is clear, and the audience is happy to invest in it, we can all totally behave as though this iPhone *was* a baby. At the point which Rosalind says 'I'm a boy', the quality of the investment in that idea from the world around her is precisely the same as the quality of investment that comes with the theatre. It's about saying 'I can be anything I want to be' and the 'fact' of that makes it 'true' ... we started in a world governed by one set of theatrical rules, which behaved much more like a conventionally naturalistic play. At the beginning, everything you saw had a kind of grounding reality, it looked like an office with lots of tables and chairs laid out ... and then we exploded these rules: the chairs and tables all pulled up and formed a massive tree sculpture, creating a forest through a change in theatrical vocabulary. (pp. 125–6)

Polly Findlay's chosen analogy – whereby the imaginative investment of the actor endows an inanimate object with a theatrical life and significance that is equal to that of the live actor – was one she found spontaneously by responding to an object in the room with us during the interview. Nonetheless, this way of articulating the actor-object relationship aligns her with the practice of Sandy Grierson's mentor Tadeusz Kantor, a practice disseminated on both sides of the Atlantic by Cricot 2 company members such as Zofia Kalinska and Ludmilla Ryba.

Ethan McSweeny's argument in partial defence of the directorial 'concept' is, I would argue, fairly representative of the view of many directors working in the larger Shakespeare producing theatres in the United States. A graduate of Columbia University, Ethan has a scrupulously detailed approach to text work, but believes that his job as a director goes somewhat beyond the elucidation of text: 'the reason concept gets a bad name is that there are some directors who do things *to* plays, and that's not very nice ... there is a big difference between doing something *to* a play and doing something *with* a play and I think we are obligated to the latter' (p. 139; emphases in the original). Greg Doran opposes this view, and regards the urge to do something *with* the plays as a misguided desire on the director's part to be original, and to assert his/her own originality at the expense of the material itself:

> The currency is in danger of being devalued, because of the amount of things we feel we have to do *with* Shakespeare, rather than *do* Shakespeare ... It requires a degree of confidence to go 'this play *works*', and the starting point shouldn't be 'how can we make this different?'. Let the starting point be the exploration, because you are different, and the actors' interpretations will be different, because they *are* different. (pp. 117–18; emphases in the original)

Tom Piper suggests that designers may find more value than directors in understanding the ways in which their work is in dialogue with other moments in the play's production history. 'I suppose all practical interpreters of Shakespeare have ... the back catalogue that one is kind of aware of, the sort of prior knowledge of seminal productions that one cannot escape consciousness of' (p. 148). However, Mike Alfreds goes further, and condemns directors

> so bent on imposing their concepts of *Lear* onto *Lear*, and focusing on those elements of the production that will show off the relevance of their interpretations, that language is often the last thing to be dealt with. It should be the first. The ideas for a production and its performance have to come *out* of the language, not be put *on* it. (pp. 92–3; emphasis in the original)

One senses that this view, though widely held, is not unchallenged. Director Renato Rocha believes that sometimes an effort must be made to make Shakespeare our contemporary:

The first step is always identifying how this story is still relevant nowadays – what it does it to us now, and what its relationship to contemporary society is. I did a lot of work with the great, famous Shakespeare plays at the beginning of my career, but after my experiences with educational and social projects in favelas and the peripheries of Brazil, my outlook changed a little. While I think it is still important that those stories be told, I'm much more interested in finding the contemporary parallels in Shakespeare's works. (p. 156)

In making his commitment to 'finding contemporary parallels in Shakespeare's works', Renato has adapted them, and used the texts to devise new works altogether: 'Our aim was to use all media, and all skills to actually create a more accessible and universal piece of theatre, that doesn't concern itself so much with narrative, but takes pains over engaging the audience on a personal level with each character' (p. 158). That said, his concern for contemporary relevance might also fit within Berry's description of more 'traditional' approaches to staging Shakespeare's texts, but it is nonetheless a very different model from that proposed by both Mike Alfreds and Greg Doran, who share an implicit belief in a kind of authenticity which comes from engaging first and foremost with the language. Though both acknowledge that individual actors choosing bespoke actions will interpret the same language differently, both also seem to be comfortable with the concept of a stable text with a defined (if not definitive) story worth the telling. This, of course, is not a million miles from the concept of there being an 'authenticity' in a directorial approach which privileges language. This concept is nicely complicated when one considers the important directorial decisions involved in cutting Shakespeare's plays.

To cut or not to cut is a vexed question indeed, and in considering it, this discussion will not concern itself with decisions involving the choice of textual variant (however important such decisions undoubtedly are) but rather with policy and practice more generally. For example, Tim Carroll weighs the value and function of each line, and maps his casting process against the same:

> I will read the play several times to work out problems of cutting and casting, deciding whether a line earns its place or not. Even if I end up not cutting anything, I read with a much better attention when I'm trying to decide what to cut and *if* to cut. When you are looking for cuts, it really makes you think about what every bit of the play is doing, and why it needs to be there. (p. 103; emphasis in the original)

Mike Alfreds advocates similar caution when cutting, and to an extent echoes Tim's principle of *lectio difficilior potior* ('the more difficult reading should stand'), though Mike is more concerned with matters of narrative clarity and thematic significance:

> Cuts should never be made merely as a contingency, nor from laziness when confronted by dense chunks of obscurity; nor to get rid of lines that would contradict your interpretation of the play. Instead, you grapple with every part of the text for its verbal meaning, its purpose in the scene, its revelation of character and motivation, its clarification of story and plot ... Otherwise, a lot of hacking takes place and the baby gets thrown out with the bath water. (p. 100)

Polly Findlay also sees the judicious editing of the script as absolutely integral to her goal of finding the 'gesture' of the play (p. 126), but in contrast to the careful weighing advocated by Mike and Tim, above, her first action with a script seems, on the face of it, a very 'extreme' act of editing:

> The first thing I would do would be to distill the play into a single sentence: this makes you articulate your own agenda with the play. Then you make sure that all of your editing decisions are tailored in such a way as to help you tell that particular story; you're using that sentence as a kind of

check and balance system to weigh against every editing decision you make. Each edit has to be in service of the pure driving line of that sentence. (p. 124)

What I find interesting here is the similarity this practice bears to Mike Alfreds's practice of naming each demarcated unit within his rehearsal script. Polly's single sentence holds exactly the same significance for her directorial choices overall, as Mike's unit titles do for his direction of the action within that unit. Polly has taken the Alfreds practice of distilling units of storytelling to its logical extreme, effectively finding in her 'sentence' a kind of unit title for the whole play. And, whereas for Mike Alfreds, each action must fulfil an objective which in turn does not contradict the unit title, for Polly, each editorial decision must produce an action which does not contradict, but rather may be folded into, the sentence/unit title of the play as a whole. From this point on, however, Polly describes a cutting practice that is a daring reinvention of the very idea of authorial intention. Her quest, as she describes it, was to decide

if *As You Like It* was written now, what would it be? And at that time I thought it would basically be *The Fast Show* ... Those scenes, particularly in the second half, don't function like typical Shakespearean scenes ... the progression in that play is to do with character development, rather than with plot. I think that what Shakespeare was probably trying to set up was something that felt much more like a series of sketches, that allowed us to see a different facet of the characters each time. (p. 126)

Once Polly had identified the 'gesture' of the show (described above), her editorial response made a significant commitment to the concept, or 'gesture', of the production:

[I]it was impossible for us to take the script of *As You Like It* as it is, and make it feel like it has the energy of a modern sketch show like *The Fast Show*; so what we did was to cut a lot of those scenes into two or three – and because there wasn't any central event, you could get away with doing that – and then splice them, so that the pace of the scene felt three or four times as fast as it might ordinarily have been. And then we borrowed bits of *All's Well That Ends Well* and a couple of other Shakespearean comedies to try and pad it out, and make the whole thing feel faster, funnier and quicker-cut. And to me that feels completely respectful of the original gesture; it's a way of bringing what that gesture was – with its full integrity – to a modern audience. (pp. 126–7)

While Polly's editing choices directly challenge the concept of authorial intention, they boldly state a commitment to a differently defined concept of authenticity: 'I think this will always unlock something more interesting than trying to honour the author's intention in what might be seen as a more traditional way … we so often see people trying replicate the performance conditions under which the play was produced, rather than trying to replicate the *sensibility* in which the play was produced' (p. 127; emphasis in the original). Polly's aims when directing *As You Like It* exceeded the strategies outlined by Ralph Berry, and it remains to be seen whether her work, along with the work of other 'new', 'emerging' or 'young' directors on the United Kingdom's most prominent stages will continue to 'explore and explode' established ways of working, or, instead, become incorporated into the 'living tradition' of staging Shakespeare's plays.

Back to the principle of action . . .

Over the course of the interviews, I had hoped to reveal some of the ways that the governing principle of action distinguishes the way an actor or a director reads a play by Shakespeare, from other ways of reading Shakespeare. In many respects, the difference between an actor's close reading and a literary-critical reading is rather subtle, and it is also no secret that many respected directors have declared a fondness for certain famous works of literary criticism. John Barton and Peter Brook were influenced, undoubtedly, by the work of Jan Kott in the 1960s, and more recently, Tim Carroll finds much value in classic critical responses to Shakespeare's plays. That said, Tim is also skeptical about their practical use in the process of bringing the plays to the stage: 'I like reading Jan Kott's *Shakespeare Our Contemporary* (1974) or Northrop Frye's essays on Shakespeare (1986), which I find inspiring, but I don't know how these feed into my work. If I knew, the work wouldn't be good' (p. 103). For Tim, the critic and director have very different purposes:

> It is important that we respect the separation of being a director of Shakespeare and of writing literary criticism of Shakespeare. I challenge the assumption that literary critics of Shakespeare *need* to take performance into account more. You can of course *read* a play like *Richard III* – and it is a beautiful thing to read – though it was of course written for the theatre, and that is no doubt part of its essential nature. But as for those critics who, as it were, point out connections between something on page 1 and page 100, which would not be noticeable in the theatre … that doesn't mean that connection isn't there, it just means that you are a chump if, in the theatre as a director, you try to bring that out. (p. 103; emphases in the original)

Tim's remarks go to the heart of the matter: critics and practitioners have different activities with a given text, performances happen in real time and the audience may not, as the reader may, pause and turn back the page for a recap. Design elements may be able to suggestively and imaginatively link moments in the text that are temporally unconnected, in ways that are interesting theatrically, but typically, the direction of narrative traffic in the theatre is clear, and one-way only. As I mentioned earlier, the main difference between the reading habits of an actor and those of general readers is the actor's tendency to read the play from the partisan perspective of the role only. This is not laziness on the part of the actor, but a form of advocacy. As Morris Carnovsky (1977, 144) puts it, '[T]he major difference between an actor's approach to a play and that of a scholar-critic is the former's inner passion and need to identify and merge sympathetically and imaginatively with the character.' Jade Anouka describes the way she collects information about the play from this unique perspective:

> I begin by getting to know the play purely from my character's point of view: first I read the scenes that my character is in, to get a sense of the character and their story. Then I look at how my character relates to other characters, what I say to and about others, and then work out who *those* people are. (p. 21; emphasis in the original)

Jade is referring to the practice of making 'character lists', a widespread practice originating from Stanislavski's system but taught in various adapted ways as 'good practice' in most drama schools. Mike Alfreds's book *Different Every Night* (2014) has been widely adopted into drama school curricula, and consequently his version of this exercise has been embraced by significant numbers of actors, including several included in this volume. For example, Eve Best recalls:

> In my second year at Oxford University, Ian McKellen was the resident Professor of Drama and I was in his group of students while he worked with us on *Uncle Vanya*. The system he taught us was a technique Mike Alfreds uses, of going through the text several times, asking different questions and making a list of direct quotes from the play that answer each question. These include: What does my character say about herself? What do I say about each of the other characters? What do the other characters say about me? (p. 28)

The information that can be gleaned from exercises like these represents for some actors a kind of distillation of the character. For others, such as Juliet Rylance, it is a place to begin the foundational work of identifying objectives:

> I begin by making three lists: what my character says about herself; what she says about others; what others say about her. This gives me a very clear idea of who she is, how she feels about herself and how she interacts with the world around her. From this list I begin to work out her super objective through the story. What drives and moves her forward through the play, how that is changed or enforced by certain events that happen in the play, and how she deals with them. (p. 73)

The work Juliet describes above will normally be done as part of the individual actor's research, prior to the start of rehearsals, but other actors find that the lists have a useful role to play in the context of group rehearsals with another popular exercise drawn from the drama school curriculum, 'hot seating', described here by Colin Hurley:

> [W]hat I say about myself, what I say about other people, what they say about me ... that's fine prep to do at home, but I find it even better if you can bring that stuff into rehearsal, and say those things to those people, to their faces in the space, maybe in a kind of 'hot seat' set-up ... saying these things to someone outside the track of a scene ... examining them out of context, some of the things you say and hear can ripple or resonate usefully ... Perhaps the cumulative effect of hearing just what everyone else in the play thinks about your character can throw things up that may not be so obvious when reading or playing the whole thing from beginning to end. It goes a long way towards the whole company carrying the world of the play together. (p. 51)

Reading through the actors' interviews, it is clear that the practice of list-making is evidently so widespread as to be almost not worth mentioning, but I have dwelt on it here, and would like to end this discussion with it, because it represents common and perhaps basic drama school practices which are not common to other learning and teaching contexts. These practices continue to be taught, because they are perceived to be helpful, and so actors continue to hone and refine these practices in their professional lives. Actors do not routinely discuss these practices because, as Colin Hurley puts it, 'I don't want to show the audience my homework' (p. 51), but until such a time as these practices are no longer deemed effective teaching tools, they will continue to shape Shakespeare 'in action' in theatres across the United States and the United Kingdom, and further afield.

I hope this collection of interviews has shown the 'living tradition' of Shakespeare in action in a celebratory light, though not an idolatrous (or indeed Bardolatrous) one: for, as Colin Hurley reminds his students, and me, acting involves practical and pragmatic choices, and actors must have '[t]ools, not rules. When they stop being useful things to consider, drop 'em, or they can become bars on a cage' (p. 51).

REFERENCES

Alfreds, M. (2014). *Different Every Night*. New York: Nick Hern Books.

Anon. (1973). William Poel Memorial Prize Charitable Objects. http://beta.charitycommission.gov.uk/charity-details/?regid=266186&subid=1 (accessed 17 June 2018).

Barton, J. (2013). *Playing Shakespeare*. London: Methuen Drama.

Berry, R. (1989). *On Directing Shakespeare: Interviews with Contemporary Directors*. London: Hamish Hamilton.

Bessell, J. (2001). *Hamlet: The 2000 Globe Season*. Globe Research Bulletin. Shakespeare's Globe. https://www.shakespearesglobe.com/uploads/files/2015/02/hamlet_2000.pdf (accessed 17 June 2018).

Block, G. (2013). *Speaking the Speech: An Actor's Guide to Shakespeare*. London: Nick Hern Books.

Caldarone, M. and Lloyd-Williams, M. (2004). *Actions: The Actors' Thesaurus*. London: Nick Hern Books.

Carnovsky, M. and Sander, P. (1977). 'The Eye of the Storm: On Playing King Lear'. *Shakespeare Quarterly* 28(2), 144–50.

Crystal, D. (2005). *Pronouncing Shakespeare*. Cambridge: Cambridge University Press.

Frye, N. (1986). *Northrop Frye on Shakespeare*. New Haven and London: Yale University Press.

Hall, P. (2014). *Shakespeare's Advice to the Players*. London: Oberon Books.

Kaiser, S. (2003). *Mastering Shakespeare: An Acting Class in Seven Scenes*. New York: Allworth Press.

Kemp, L. (1982). *Flowers: A Pantomime for Jean Genet* [video]. Teatro Parioli Rome: Lindsay Kemp Dance Company.

Kott, J. (1974). *Shakespeare Our Contemporary*. New York: W. W. Norton & Company.

Levitkin, D. (2007). *This Is Your Brain on Music*. London: Penguin Books Ltd.

Merlin, B. (2011). *The Complete Stanislavsky Toolkit*. London: Nick Hern Books.

Purcell, S. (2017). *Shakespeare in the Theatre: Mark Rylance at the Globe*. London: Bloomsbury.

Rokison, A. (2009). *Shakespearean Verse Speaking*. Cambridge: Cambridge University Press.

Schmidt, A. and Sarrazin, G. (2017). *Shakespeare Lexicon*. Eastford, CT: Martino Fine Books.

Stanislavsky, C. and Hapgood, E. R. (2013). *An Actor Prepares*. Bloomsbury Revelations. London: Bloomsbury.

Stanislavsky, C. and Hapgood, E. R. (2013). *Building a Character*. Bloomsbury Revelations. London: Bloomsbury.

Strasberg, L. (1969). 'Speaking Freely', interview by Edwin Newman. NBC News Series. Gordon Skene Sound Collection, 14 December. https://pastdaily.com/wp-content/uploads/2015/09/Lee-Strasberg-Speaking-Freely-Dec.-14-1969.mp3 (accessed 19 June 2018).

Works by Shakespeare

Cymbeline. Ed. V. Wayne. Arden Third Series. London: Bloomsbury Arden Shakespeare, 2017.

Hamlet (The Second Quarto, 1604–5). Ed. A. Thompson and N. Taylor. Arden Third Series. London: Bloomsbury Arden Shakespeare, 2006.

King Henry V. Ed. T. W. Craik. Arden Third Series. London: Bloomsbury Arden Shakespeare, 1995.

King Richard II. Ed. C. R. Forker. Arden Third Series. London: Bloomsbury Arden Shakespeare, 2002.

Love's Labour's Lost. Ed. H. R. Woudhuysen. Arden Third Series. London: Bloomsbury Arden Shakespeare, 1998.

Macbeth. Ed. S. Clark and P. Mason. Arden Third Series. London: Bloomsbury Arden Shakespeare, 2015.

Measure for Measure. Ed. J. W. Lever. Arden Second Series. London: Bloomsbury Arden Shakespeare, 1967.

A Midsummer Night's Dream. Ed. S. Chaudhuri. Arden Third Series. London: Bloomsbury Arden Shakespeare, 2017.

Much Ado About Nothing. Ed. C. McEachern. Arden Third Series. London: Bloomsbury Arden Shakespeare, 2005.

Othello. Revised edn. Ed. E. A. J. Honigmann, intro. A. Thompson. Arden Third Series. London: Bloomsbury Arden Shakespeare, 2016.

Romeo and Juliet. Ed. R. Weiss. Arden Third Series. London: Bloomsbury Arden Shakespeare, 2012.

Shakespeare's Sonnets. Ed. K. Duncan-Jones. Arden Third Series. London: Bloomsbury Arden Shakespeare, 2010.

The Tempest. Ed. V. M. Vaughan and A. T. Vaughan. Arden Third Series. London: Bloomsbury Arden Shakespeare, 2011.

Titus Andronicus. Ed. J. Bate. Arden Third Series. London: Bloomsbury Arden Shakespeare, 1995.

Twelfth Night. Ed. K. Elam. Arden Third Series. London: Bloomsbury Arden Shakespeare, 2008.

The Winter's Tale. Ed. J. Pitcher. Arden Third Series. London: Bloomsbury Arden Shakespeare, 2010.

SUGGESTED FURTHER READING

The selected list of titles below is intended to guide readers towards the kinds of publications most used in drama schools at the time of writing. As such the list is not exhaustive, but emphasizes practical knowledge and application.

Acting

Adler, S. (2000). *The Art of Acting*. New York: Applause Books.

Benedetti, J. (2000). *Stanislavski: An Introduction*. London: Methuen.

Benedetti, J. (2008). *An Actor's Work*. London: Routledge.

Caldarone, M. and Lloyd-Williams, M. (2004). *Actions: The Actors' Thesaurus*. London: Nick Hern Books.

Chekhov, M. (2002). *To the Actor: On the Technique of Acting*. London: Routledge.

Donnellan, D. (2005). *The Actor and the Target*. London: Nick Hern Books.

Hagen, U. (1991). *Challenge for the Actor*. New York: Scribner.

Hagen, U. and Frankel, H. (1973). *Respect for Acting*. New York: Macmillan.

Hodge, A. (2000). *20th Century Actor Training*. London: Routledge.

Johnstone, K. (1987). *Impro*. London: Methuen.

Mamet, D. (1998). *True and False*. London: Faber and Faber.

Meisner, S. (1990). *On Acting*. London: Vintage.

Merlin, B. (2001). *Beyond Stanislavsky*. London: Nick Hern Books.

Merlin, B. (2011). *The Complete Stanislavsky Toolkit*. London: Nick Hern Books.

Richards, T. (1995). *At Work with Grotowski on Physical Action*. London: Routledge.

Stanislavsky, C. and Hapgood, E. R. (2013). *An Actor Prepares*. Bloomsbury Revelations. London: Bloomsbury.

Stanislavsky, C. and Hapgood, E. R. (2013). *Building a Character*. Bloomsbury Revelations. London: Bloomsbury.

Stanislavsky, C. and Hapgood, E. R. (2013). *Creating a Role*. Bloomsbury Revelations. London: Bloomsbury.

Movement

Allain, P. (2002). *The Art of Stillness: The Theatre Practice of Tadashi Suzuki*. London: Methuen.

Callery, D. (2001). *Through the Body*. London: Nick Hern Books.

Dennis, A. (2002). *The Articulate Body: The Physical Training of the Actor*. London: Nick Hern Books.

Feldenkrais, M. (1990). *Awareness through Movement*. London: Penguin.

Laban, R. and Ullman, R. (1988). *Mastery of Movement*. New Jersey: Northcote House.

Lecoq, J., Carasso, J., Lallias, J. and Bradby, D. (2014). *The Moving Body*. London: Bloomsbury Methuen Drama.

Newlove, J. (1993). *Laban for Actors and Dancers: Putting Laban's Movement Theory into Practice*. London: Nick Hern Books.

Potter, N. (2002). *Movement for Actors*. London: Allworth Communications.

Wigman, M. (1996). *The Languages of Dance*. Ohio: Wesleyan University Press.

Directing

Alfreds, M. (2007). *Different Every Night: Freeing the Actor*. London: Nick Hern Books.

Artaud, A. (2000). *The Theatre and Its Double*. London: Grove/Atlantic.

Berry, R. (1989). *On Directing Shakespeare: Interviews with Contemporary Directors*. London: Hamish Hamilton.

Bogart, A. and Landau, T. (2005). *The Viewpoints Book: A Practical Guide to Viewpoints and Composition*. New York: Theatre Communications Group.

Brook, P. (1972). *The Empty Space*. London: Penguin Books.

Brook, P. (2002). *Evoking (and Forgetting) Shakespeare*. London: Nick Hern Books.

Mitchell, K. (2008). *The Director's Craft: A Handbook for the Theatre*. London: Taylor & Francis.

Trevis, D. (2011). *Being a Director: A Life in Theatre*. London: Routledge.

Voice, verse and text

Barton, J. (2013). *Playing Shakespeare*. London: Methuen Drama.

Berry, C. (2001). *Text in Action*. London: Virgin Books.

Berry, C. (2000). *The Actor and the Text*. London: Virgin Books.

Block, G. (2013). *Speaking the Speech: An Actor's Guide to Shakespeare*. London: Nick Hern Books.

Crystal, D. and Crystal, B. (2002). *Shakespeare's Words*. London: Penguin.

Fogerty, E. (1929). *Speaking English Verse*. London: Dent.

Hall, P. (2003). *Shakespeare's Advice to the Players*. London: Oberon Books.

Kaiser, S. (2003). *Mastering Shakespeare: An Acting Class in Seven Scenes*. New York: Allworth Press.

Lessac, A. (1997). *Use and Training of the Human Voice: A Biodynamic Approach to Vocal Life*. New York: Mayfield.

Linklater, K. (1976). *Freeing the Natural Voice*. New York: D B Publishers.

Linklater, K. (1992). *Freeing Shakespeare's Voice*. New York: Theatre Communications Group.

McCallion, M. (1988). *The Voice Book*. London: Faber and Faber.

Noble, A. (2010). *How to Do Shakespeare*. London: Routledge.

Rodenburg, P. (2002). *Speaking Shakespeare*. London: Methuen.

Rodenburg, P. (2017). *Need for Words*. London: Methuen.

Rokison, A. (2009). *Shakespearean Verse Speaking*. Cambridge: Cambridge University Press.

Schmidt, A. and Sarrazin, G. (2017). *Shakespeare Lexicon*. Eastford, CT: Martino Fine Books.

Lighting design

Cadena, R. (2010). *Automated Lighting: The Art and Science of Moving Light in Theatre, Live Performance, and Entertainment.* 2nd edn. Amsterdam: Taylor and Francis.

Jackman, J. (2010). *Lighting for Digital Video and Television.* 3rd edn. Amsterdam: Taylor and Francis.

Moran, N. (2007). *Performance Lighting Design: How to Light for the Stage, Concerts, Exhibitions and Live Events.* London: A & C Black.

Moran, N. (2017). *The Right Light: Interviews with Contemporary Lighting Designers.* London: Macmillan Education.

Mort, S. (2011). *Stage Lighting: The Technicians' Guide: An On-the-Job Reference Tool Plus DVD Video Resources.* London: Methuen.

Pilbrow, R., Chiang, D., Read, J. B., Bryan, R. and Gaskell, L. (2008). *Stage Lighting Design: The Art, the Craft, the Life.* London: Nick Hern Books.

Schiller, B. (2011). *The Automated Lighting Programmer's Handbook.* 2nd edn. Amsterdam: Elsevier, Taylor and Francis.

Scenography

Baugh, C. (2013). *Theatre, Performance and Technology: The Development and Transformation of Scenography.* 2nd edn. Basingstoke: Palgrave Macmillan.

Burnett, K. (2007). *Collaborators: UK Design for Performance 2003–2007.* London: Society of British Theatre Designers.

Howard, P. (2009). *What Is Scenography?* 2nd edn. London: Routledge.

McKinney, J. and Butterworth, P. (eds) (2009). *The Cambridge Introduction to Scenography.* Cambridge: Cambridge University Press.

Sound design

Biederman, R. and Pattison P. (2014). *Basic Live Sound Reinforcement: A Practical Guide for Starting Live Audio.* New York: Taylor & Francis.

Collison, D. (2008). *The Sound of Theatre: A History.* Eastbourne: Plasa.

Davis, G. and Jones, R. (1989). *The Sound Reinforcement Handbook.* 2nd edn. Milwaukee, WI: Hal Leonard Corporation.

Kaye, D. and LeBrecht, J. (2009). *Sound and Music for the Theatre: The Art and Technique of Design.* 3rd edn. Oxford: Taylor and Francis.

Leonard, J. A. (2001). *Theatre Sound.* London: A & C Black.

Shakespeare in performance

Bennett, S. and Carson, C. (eds) (2013). *Shakespeare beyond English: A Global Experiment.* Cambridge: Cambridge University Press.

Brown, J. R. (ed.) (2008). *The Routledge Companion to Directors' Shakespeare.* London: Routledge.

Brown, J. R. (ed.) and Ewert, K. (associate ed.) (2012). *The Routledge Companion to Directors' Shakespeare.* London: Routledge.

Carson, C. and Karim-Cooper, F. (eds) (2008). *Shakespeare's Globe: A Theatrical Experiment.* Cambridge: Cambridge University Press.

Davies, O. F. (2007). *Performing Shakespeare: Preparation, Rehearsal, Performance.* London: Nick Hern Books.

Dobson, M. (2006). *Performing Shakespeare's Tragedies Today: The Actor's Perspective.* Cambridge: Cambridge University Press.

Purcell, S. (2017). *Shakespeare in the Theatre: Mark Rylance at the Globe.* London: Bloomsbury.

Rutter, C. and Evans, F. (1988). *Clamorous Voices: Shakespeare's Women Today.* London: The Women's Press.

Sher, A. (2004). *Year of the King.* London: Nick Hern Books.

ABOUT THE AUTHOR

Jaq Bessell's career began at the Guthrie Theater in Minneapolis, and she was head of research at Shakespeare's Globe during Mark Rylance's tenure, where she developed a keen interest in verse-speaking techniques. She has directed productions of plays by Shakespeare and modern playwrights in New York and London and regional theatres across the United States. She has taught in conservatoires on both coasts of the United States, and now leads the MA/MFA Acting programme at the Guildford School of Acting, where she is director of postgraduate studies. She has published extensively on Shakespeare in performance, in chapters and articles which stem from her work as a director and teacher of acting, and she regularly leads workshops in verse-speaking, audition technique and the Viewpoints in the United Kingdom and Europe. In 2016 she and the renowned dancer and director Lindsay Kemp co-directed *Romeo and Juliet* for the Verona Shakespeare Festival, a project which resulted in the formation of NOMA, an Italian dance theatre company, with whom she has developed a somatic approach to classical text which exceeds the boundaries of language and disciplines.

INDEX